Today's Guide to
RETIREMENT PLANNING

A Resource for Adults Ages 50 and Over

DAVID HAYS AND DOUG HUGHES

authorHOUSE®

AuthorHouse™
1663 Liberty Drive
Bloomington, IN 47403
www.authorhouse.com
Phone: 1 (800) 839-8640

© 2019 David Hays and Doug Hughes. All rights reserved.

No part of this book may be reproduced, stored in a retrieval system, or transmitted by any means without the written permission of the author.

Published by AuthorHouse 07/31/2019

ISBN: 978-1-7283-1911-7 (sc)
ISBN: 978-1-7283-1933-9 (e)

Print information available on the last page.

Any people depicted in stock imagery provided by Getty Images are models, and such images are being used for illustrative purposes only.
Certain stock imagery © Getty Images.

This book is printed on acid-free paper.

Because of the dynamic nature of the Internet, any web addresses or links contained in this book may have changed since publication and may no longer be valid. The views expressed in this work are solely those of the author and do not necessarily reflect the views of the publisher, and the publisher hereby disclaims any responsibility for them.

Securities offered through J.W. Cole Financial, Inc. (JWC), Member FINRA/SIPC

Advisory Services offered through J.W. Cole Advisors, Inc. (JWCA) and/or Comprehensive Financial Consultants Institutional, Inc (CFCI). Comprehensive Financial Consultants and CFCI/JWC/JWCA are unaffiliated entities.

The opinions expressed by the authors of Today's Guide to Retirement Planning should not be construed as specific investment, legal or tax advice.

All economic and performance information is historical and not indicative of future results. Investing may involve the risk of loss of principal.

Any tax advice in this book is not intended to be used by any person for the purpose of avoiding US Federal or State Tax – penalties that may be imposed on such person. Seek advice from their tax advisor or legal counsel on topics that arise from the show.

The authors of this book are not providing legal or tax advice, nothing should be construed as a solicitation or an offer to buy securities.

CONTENTS

Introduction ix

1 Planning For Retirement 1
2 Needs And Expenses In Retirement 15
3 Retirement Hurdles 23
4 Available Income Sources 37
5 Retirement Plan Distributions 81
6 Investments 101
7 Insurance, Risk Management And Asset Protection 129
8 Estate Planning 149

About The Authors... 165

INTRODUCTION

Are you thinking about retiring in the next few years or already are? This book is designed as a resource guide for you! "Today's Guide to Retirement Planning" is the culmination of our nearly 45 years of combined experience working with retirees and pre-retirees. This book isn't designed to be a "do it yourself guide", but a resource to help you become better equipped as you talk with a financial professional.

The Baby-Boom generation has changed and influenced everything from the hula-hoop to the Ford Mustang and retirement will be no different. This isn't your parent's or grandparent's retirement; this is your retirement! Being fulfilled during retirement isn't all about money, it's about relationships, staying connected, and being healthy. This book is designed to help you start the necessary conversations and help you think of the things you should be considering as the next chapter of your life begins.

So take your time as you read through this book, skip around if you want, and if you have any questions, please don't hesitate to reach out to either of us though our website: www.cfci.us.

Thank you to our families for their encouragement and support, and to our clients who have given us the opportunity to be of service to them – enjoy!

Authors,
David Hays & Doug Hughes

> "The three big risks in retirement planning are that you live too long, die too soon, or get too sick or hurt to work."
> -Doug Hughes

1
PLANNING FOR RETIREMENT

Recently a married couple in their early 60s sat down in our office and began talking about their retirement dreams. The couple—we'll call them John and Mary Smith—were nearing retirement after working for more than four decades. John labored as a certified public accountant for several companies, Mary as a high school English teacher.

They were excited about their future, feeling confident that income from Social Security and a $750,000 nest egg would enable them to embark upon a new chapter in their lives. For them, retirement did not mean rocking chairs and TV reruns; siestas and shuffleboard. It meant a gateway to a promising new life brimming with activity and adventure.

John wanted to fulfill a pair of long-harbored dreams—learning Spanish and woodworking. Mary could hardly wait to launch a neighborhood supper club and begin volunteering with a child advocacy group. Together, they spoke with grade school giddiness about their plans to do more traveling, and learn how to ballroom dance.

As they unveiled their retirement aspirations, we couldn't help but notice the sparkle in their eyes and vibrancy in their voices. Together, they had worked more than 80 years in their professions. Now, as the curtain was about to close on their careers, they saw their lives spreading before them like a golden expressway—filled with boundless possibilities.

The Smiths represent a new breed of retirees, those who see their elder years not as a time to sit on the sidelines, but to stay in the game. A time to spread their wings and live in a way that fuels their passions and personalities. A time to make new friends, set new goals, and engage in new activities that foster a sense of meaning and purpose in their lives.

People like the Smiths crave an independent lifestyle that blends pleasure with purpose. They see retirement as the dawning of a new era, one overflowing with fresh challenges and opportunities.

Traditional view of retirement

This new take on retirement represents a distinct departure from the traditional view of retirement— namely that it's a ticket to Take-It-Easyville. This view, largely embraced by our parents' generation, held that retirement was a time to celebrate the cessation of work—sleeping in late and sipping lemonade while lounging in a hammock. The golden years were seen primarily as an extended vacation.

Our parents' retirement planning often focused solely on money—accumulating a large enough income stream through company pensions and Social Security to spend their retirement years in leisure and relative comfort. But they did not give much thought to how they would live those years, and as a result they often felt adrift and rudderless—struggling to find purpose in their lives and fill their days with meaningful activities.

To a large extent, this traditional retirement perspective was held by people who worked at the same company for many years, then retired at 65 and began receiving Social Security and a comfortable pension based on a formula that took into account their salary and years of service. They didn't have to put a great deal of thought and planning into their retirement income because it was based on fairly predictable formulas. And for the most part, they didn't worry about getting their financial affairs in order until they were nearing the end of their lives.

Today, there certainly are some people who still embrace the traditional retirement view. Once they put in their 35 years with the company and get the gold watch, they want to do little more than play golf and chill out. They have reached the finish line and they're done. There's nothing wrong with that mindset, but we've found over the years that our clients who "retire to" rather than "retire from" tend to find more fulfillment in their golden years.

We've also seen some folks who begin their retirement devoid of dreams, but after being swarmed with requests to babysit grandchildren at a moment's notice and teach Sunday School and take meals to the sick, they decide they want something more out of retirement. They start thinking about things they've always wanted to do, but never had the time to do, and begin taking steps to turn those longings into reality.

Why things have changed

Today things are different. In our company we find that 75 to 80 percent of our clients have this new view of retirement. National surveys reflect the same trend. Only 22 percent of those 55 and older say they view retirement as a "winding down" or "extended vacation;" and when

50-to-75-year-olds were surveyed, 70 percent saw retirement as a time to "stay active and begin a new chapter."[1]

But why this shift in thinking? Part of the answer is that peoples' working histories today look far different that they did a generation ago. Nowadays more people are self-employed, and most of them work for 4, 5, or 6 companies (often in differing capacities) during their careers. As a result, many retire without a significant pension—or no pension at all. And because many folks today are charting a more self-directed career path, they tend to take a more active role in their retirement planning. They have a tendency to take greater initiative in crafting a more active and independent retirement lifestyle.

But there are other factors at play. Due to a heightened awareness of the importance of exercise and a nutritious diet—in concert with significant advances in medicine—people today are enjoying longer and healthier lives. Indeed, Baby Boomers can legitimately expect to spend one third to one fourth of their lives in retirement. When Social Security was established in 1935, the average life expectancy of Americans was 61. Today, the average Baby Boomer will live to 87.ii[2]

What's more, Americans are retiring earlier. Sixty-five percent are hanging it up before age 65.[3]

Early retirement, coupled with longer life spans, means those who focus full-time on fun during that segment of their lives run the risk of becoming bored. Nearly 80 percent of boomers expect to work in some

---

[1] Life Options Institute's Baby Boomer Facts.
[2] U.S. Census Bureau.
[3] 2012 survey by the Employee Benefit Research Institute and Matthew Greenwald and Associates.

capacity after they retire. Fifty-one percent plan to work full-time, and 28 percent predict they will work part-time.[4]

New retirement opportunities

The new view of retirement affords you with a wealth of fresh opportunities. You may want to continue to work for pay, either full-or part-time. You may want to volunteer with a charity; renew old friendships or foster new ones; do some traveling; or become involved in a service club, faith congregation, hobby, or recreational activity. You may want to reinvent yourself by starting a new career, launching a business, or going back to school.

To help you experience the kind of retirement you really want, it is important to remember that retirement planning should not be focused solely on money. Sure, financial security will widen the scope of your post-career possibilities, but money alone does not guarantee a full, rich and purpose-driven life. It doesn't define your life now, or what it will be in retirement. And contrary to the messages we see in the media every day, you can have a fulfilling retirement without a bank account bulging at the seams. Have you seen the TV commercial featuring folks riding a bicycle, clipping the hedges, and talking with a neighbor—each with a dollar figure attached to their torsos? It's suggesting that if we can just expand our nest egg up to that magical number, we will be happy and fulfilled in retirement.

But no dollar amount can ensure inner satisfaction once we retire. That's because there are many other factors that will determine your

---

[4] "Wall Street Cheat Sheet," a USA Today content partner.

happiness quotient. Take the social component, for example. Surveys show the most powerful predictor of satisfaction in retirement is a person's social network, not his or her wealth. One such survey found that two-thirds of Baby Boomers predict their happiness in retirement will stem primarily from their relationships with family and friends.

If it's true that what gives life its richest texture are social connections, then your retirement plan should provide opportunities for you to maintain and enhance your relationships with your spouse, children, grandchildren, and neighbors. It should allow you to deepen your long-held friendships, forge new friendships, and rekindle old friendships.

One of the beautiful things about retirement is that you have the luxury of thinking outside the box. Recently I (Doug) was on a Caribbean cruise and met a retired couple that were on their 23rd cruise. They told me they moved to Florida after retiring—where they kept their bags packed and waited for their travel agent to call them whenever he came across a good deal on a cruise. They were enjoying this particular 5-night tropical excursion for a total of $400 between them because they'd booked it at the last minute to take advantage of a special offer. They explained that because someone else did their laundry, cooked their meals, and washed the dishes, they were free to enjoy one another's company and do whatever they wished. And by eliminating other expenses such as car gas, restaurant bills, and utility costs, they found it was less expensive for them to live on a cruise ship than in their home.

New retirement responsibilities

But there's another side to the "new retirement" coin. Facing the prospect of having more years in retirement—not to mention more financial and lifestyle choices during those years—brings with it more responsibilities.

The traditional retirement planning process was fairly easy. You would buy some life insurance from an agent, a handful of stocks from a broker, and some certificates of deposit at a bank. You then factored in your guaranteed monthly income from Social Security and your pension—and waited for those checks to begin arriving in the mailbox upon retirement.

But with changes to Social Security looming on the horizon and fewer and fewer companies offering pensions, you must become more engaged in your financial future. You have to spend more time educating yourself so you can make informed decisions and investment choices in a volatile economic environment. You have to evaluate where you are financially right now, then develop a comprehensive plan designed to make your retirement dreams come true.

The plan must have a cohesive investment strategy that incorporates a balanced mix of financial products—forming a coordinated portfolio that can provide you with a reliable lifetime income stream. It must clearly delineate where your income will be coming from and whether or not it's contractually guaranteed, which investments will pay what kind of interest or dividends and how often, and how a variable annuity might work in conjunction with an income annuity. The days of saying, "I'll just put away $500 a month, get an 18 percent return, and be a millionaire in retirement" are gone.

The plan must be comprehensive, containing a number of built-in contingencies that address all kinds of unforeseen scenarios—such as the loss of a job, health problems, disability, death, or changes to Social Security benefits.

There's an old saying in the financial planning world—"The three big risks in retirement planning are that you live too long, die too soon, or get too sick or hurt to work." A comprehensive plan must account for all three of those possibilities.

One more thing: even the best of retirement plans can't be carved in stone. It must be flexible. Due to an ever-evolving economy and the changing circumstances of life, you will need to periodically review your plan and make adjustments.

Start planning now

Whether you possess a new or traditional perspective on how you'll live your elder years, the time to start planning for retirement is now! Your happiness and fulfillment may depend on how well you map out and follow a plan that will take you where you want to go. If you develop a clear picture of what it will take to bring optimum fulfillment to your retirement years, you can start planning the financial strategies you'll need to turn that picture into reality.

You may feel you're just too busy to develop a clear vision of your retirement lifestyle, but just winging it is not good enough. It's like the old saying goes: "If you aim at nothing, you'll hit it every time." You need a plan.

We recently were reminded of this reality when Indiana University offered its employees age 60 and over an early retirement buy-out with a lump sum payment. Our office was inundated with 60-somethings who wanted to discuss the wisdom of accepting the offer. We found there was dramatic difference between those who'd been working with a financial advisor and planning for retirement and those who hadn't. The ones who'd been in planning mode for several years were concerned, but also cool and collected about their impending decision. Those who hadn't given their retirement much thought were visibly stressed out. The looks of concern etched on their faces were palpable— highlighting the needless emotional turmoil folks experience when they fail to formulate a retirement plan.

Taking self-inventory

We want to give you a simple exercise you can use to help you jump start the retirement planning process. It's a series of simple questions about your values, interests, and retirement expectations. Your answers—or the answers of you and your spouse—can help you design your own individual plan for living a meaningful and fulfilling retirement.

This exercise can be particularly helpful to married couples by helping them be certain they're envisioning the same kind of lifestyle in retirement. To assist you in developing a clearer vision of what you truly want your retirement to look like, we encourage you to answer the questions posed in the following nine categories—education and growth, health and fitness, leisure and recreation, spirituality, career and work, financial, home, relationships, and community and charity.

The queries are not meant to be comprehensive, but will hopefully trigger your thought processes and crystallize your plans and objectives in retirement. If you're married, it's helpful if you and your spouse answer the questions individually, then discuss your answers together.

These discussions can uncover conflicting attitudes or expectations that could lead to trouble down the retirement road. Take the matter of risk tolerance, for example. Over the years, we've found that many husbands and wives differ a great deal in their tolerance for financial risk. This often causes tension and conflict within the marriage. If the husband is a risk taker and his wife is not, he might beat his chest when the market is bullish—telling his wife he made the right investment decision. But if the market plunges, the wife might chastise him for being too much of a gambler with their life savings. This unending "blame game" can drive a wedge between them, poisoning their relationship.

You may find that you and your partner have differing thoughts about long-term health care insurance. A husband may feel it's too pricey, but if the wife has seen her parents' lifesavings eaten away when her mother had to enter a nursing home and fork over $75,000 a year for custodial care, she may be convinced long-term health care insurance is a must.

How you want to spend your leisure time must be discussed. Do you want to fish three times a week? Does your spouse plan to spend lots of time with the grandkids? Do both of you want to go on a cruise once a year? If so, the two of you can budget a sum of money each year to cover that expense.

How about your home? We often see people who move into a smaller home or condo when they retire, but oftentimes that smaller home is not necessarily a cheaper home—especially if it has the granite kitchen counter top you always longed for and the master bedroom of your dreams.

The unknowns are endless. Do you want to re-locate to be closer to your children and grandchildren, or is your mind set on snow birding to Florida each winter? Do you want to do more volunteer work or go on short-term mission trips with your church?

And here's a big one. How much financial support, if any, do you plan on giving your children and/or parents? Many of you are part of the "sandwich generation," providing care or financial support to your aging parents while doing the same for your grown children. The 2008 stock market crash cut the value of many elderly people's nest eggs in half, and the ensuing recession left scores of 20-somethings searching in vain for a job. Maybe that's why today's parents feel the age at which their children must be out of their house for good is 27—much higher than the age our parents would have said it's time for their kids to leave the nest.[5]

So whether you're single or married, divorced or widowed, never married or soon-to-be married, it's time to tackle some of these retirement questions. But we must issue a word of caution. It's critical that you answer the questions truthfully. You need to be honest about what floats your boat, and just as importantly, what doesn't. Without brutal candor, this quiz will be an exercise in futility.

GROWTH AND CONTINUING EDUCATION

- I want to explore new things.
- I want to learn several new things.
- I plan to educate myself on these things.

---

[5] 2013 survey by Coldwell Banker Real Estate.

- I want to go back to college.
- I want a new career.

FITNESS AND HEALTH

- I want to take steps to maintain good fitness and health.
- I plan to continue my fitness activities and/or sports that I'm currently involved in.
- I want to—or have already—bought long-term healthcare insurance.
- I plan to take up a new fitness activity or sport.

RELAX AND ENJOY

- I plan to do a relaxing activity once per week.
- I want to take a vacation once a year.
- I want to attend the fine arts.
- I plan to continue enjoying a particular hobby I'm now involved in.
- I would like to participate in recreational activities with others.

FAITH

- I want to grow in my faith.
- I want to volunteer and support the cause.
- I want an estate plan to include a monetary gift to the cause.
- I plan to continue contributing money to support spiritual causes.
- My estate plan includes financial gifts to spiritual causes.

WORK

- I don't have any desire to work.

- I want to volunteer or work for pay.
- I want a new career.
- I need a career change.
- I already know how I will answer the question— "So what do you do?"

MONEY

- I know what matters to me when it comes to money.
- I believe that Social Security will be there for me.
- I am worried about not having enough money.
- I think I have enough money to do what I want.
- I plan on spending less in retirement.
- I plan on spending more in retirement.

HOME

- I plan to downsize my home.
- As long as I am able, I plan to maintain my own home.
- I need to remodel my home.
- I plan to do a reverse mortgage.
- I want to move.

RELATIONSHIPS

- I am supporting my parents or children.
- I plan on visiting my children/grandchildren.
- I plan to renew old friendships.
- Retirement may cause stress on my marriage.
- I want to leave my family and friends money when I die.

VOLUNTEERING AND CHARITY

- I want to contribute to my community (time/money).
- I want to get involved with a favorite charity.
- When I die I want to leave money to my charity.
- I want to give money to charity upon my death.
- I see the tax benefit of giving to a charity.

"You can't take growth to the grocery store and spend it."
-David Hays

2

NEEDS AND EXPENSES IN RETIREMENT

Most of us are optimists. That's why the majority of pre-retirement Americans say they are confident about their financial futures. One survey found that 52 percent of workers are either "very" or "somewhat" confident they will have enough money to live comfortably—not extravagantly but comfortably—throughout retirement; and 71 percent of workers are "very" or "somewhat" confident they'll have enough money to take care of their basic expenses throughout retirement.[6]

But the survey unearthed this startling statistic—a paltry 42 percent of workers said they or their spouses have tried to calculate how much they will need to save to meet their needs and desires in retirement. Granted, figuring out how much money you'll need to make your golden years golden is not an easy task. That's because you have to plug variables, not constants, into your retirement income equation. But there are some undeniable trends that can take a sizable slice out of your retirement income and chip away the purchasing power of that income. In this chapter we are going to look at some of those trends.

---

[6] 2012 Survey by Employee Benefit Research Institute and Matthew Greenwald and Associates.

People are retiring earlier

In general people are retiring earlier. A survey of two different groups of Americans—those who were still working and those who'd already retired—found that only 24 percent of the workers surveyed said they planned to retire before age 65, but 65 percent of the retirees surveyed said they actually ended their careers prior to age 65[7]. Another survey confirmed those findings, showing that while the average American worker predicts he or she will work until age 67, 60 percent of recently retired Americans say they had to leave the work force sooner than they'd planned.[8]

Why the wide disparity between workers' predictions and their retirement realities? There are several reasons, ranging from health problems or disabilities to the downsizing or closing of one's company.

Today an increasing number of companies in cost-cutting mode are trimming their work force by offering their employees early retirement buy outs. This usually involves giving them a lump sum payment rather than a lifetime pension. These companies figure that on average this will save them money in the long run, and they're right. But by bolstering their bottom line they are compromising the long-term financial security of their workers once they retire.

---

[7] 2012 Survey by Employee Benefit Research Institute and Matthew Greenwald and Associates.

[8] 2013 Survey by PNC Financial Services Group.

People are living longer

People today are living longer than ever before. That's generally a good thing, which is why you don't see any "early-death" activists marching in Washington D.C, chanting for shorter life spans. But this longevity, coupled with earlier retirements, means today's pre-retirees need to do a better job of financial planning to ensure they don't outlive their money.

The average life expectancy of a 55-year-old male today is 80, and an average 55-year-old female can expect to live to 83.4. [9] If you're an average 65-year-old man today, you can expect to live to age 82.3, and an average woman the same age is expected to live to 85. A 75-year-old male has a life expectancy of 85.7, whereas an average 75-year-old woman should live to 87.6.[10]

If you're among the 23 percent of American workers who retire before age 55, you can expect to live a quarter of a century or more in retirement before you die. That's a long time for your money to last, especially if you haven't been planning for retirement. [11]

Insidious inflation

One of the most feared enemies of people living on a fixed income is inflation. It's an insidious foe, slowly but inexorably increasing the cost

---

[9] 2012 Report by the U.S. Department of Health and Human Services and Centers for Disease Control and Prevention.

[10] 2012 Report by the U.S. Department of Health and Human Services and Centers for Disease Control and Prevention.

[11] 2012 Survey by Employee Benefit Research Institute and Matthew Greenwald and Associates.

of goods and services over the years, thus eroding the purchasing power of your hard-earned dollars. It can eat away your nest egg in the same way a termite noiselessly gnaws holes in the foundation of your home. Though no one can precisely predict the future rate of inflation, past inflationary trends can give us a good indication, enabling us to estimate with some measure of confidence the cost of goods and services in the years ahead.

The inflation rate (known as the Consumer Price Index) over the period—2003-2012—averaged 2.4 percent. When you examine the period—1993 through 2002—the 20-year inflation rate is also 2.4 percent.[12] Though at first glance an inflation rate of 2.4 percent may not seem particularly problematic, over time it can wreak havoc with the purchasing power of retirees' money.

Assuming an annual inflation rate of 3 percent (slightly higher than the historical 2.4 percent average), it will take $1.34 cents 10 years from now to buy what $1 will purchase today. Twenty years from today, it will require $1.80 to buy what you can now get for $1; and 30 years down the road it will take a whopping $2.43.

Here's another way to look at it. Still assuming the same 3 percent inflation rate, 10 years from now you would need $6,720 to buy the same amount of goods and services that $5,000 will buy today. In 20 years you would need $9,030 to maintain the same purchasing power, and in 30 years you'd need $12,135.

Now let's flip things around and examine how much future purchasing power $5,000 in today's dollars will have in the years ahead, assuming a 3 percent annual inflation rate. Ten years from now that $5,000 will be

---

[12] U.S. Bureau of Labor Statistics.

able to buy only $3,720 in goods and services. In 20 years its purchasing power will dwindle to $2,769, and in 30 years it will shrink to $2,060.

DIFFERENT INFLATION RATES

In the United States the Consumer Price Index is a measure of the average change over time in the prices paid by consumers for a market basket of goods and services. While economists frequently talk about the Consumer Price Index and its impact on everyday Americans, few of them point out that there are actually three other CPIs. One is the CPIU (Consumer Price Index for Urban Dwellers), which tends to run higher for those who live in big cities than it does for suburban and rural residents. Another is the CPIW (Consumer Price Index for Wage Earners), which measures the cost of goods and services for the average American worker. Then there's the CPIE (Consumer Price Index for the Elderly), which tracks the cost of goods and services for the average 65-year-old American, and usually runs at 4 to 5 percent.

When planning for your retirement, you should also consider your *personal* Consumer Price Index, which hinges on the types of things you typically spend money on. Take restaurants, for example. If you prefer to eat at Olive Garden and Red Lobster, the annual inflation rate will add $2 to $3 to your bill each year. If you like eating at McDonalds, your average bill might go up 40 to 50 cents a year. Do you like to vacation on a cruise liner or in an RV? Buy new cars or used? Drink chardonnay or Bud Light? These lifestyle choices will impact your spending, and as a result, your personal CPI.

INFLATION AND INCOME TAXES

As we've shown, inflation can do some serious harm to your investment returns and buying power. But inflation has an evil cousin—the Tax Man. Together, this tandem of trouble-making factors can do double damage to your portfolio and purchasing power.

Let's assume, for example, that you have a $100,000 investment with an annualized return of 5 percent, earning you $5,000 a year. If we assume you're in a 25 percent federal income tax bracket, you will owe an income tax of $1,250 on that $5,000, reducing your earnings to $3,750. But that's not all. Assuming inflation is 3 percent, you will lose another $3,113 in actual purchasing power on your $103,750 in a year's time. When you subtract income taxes and inflationary damage from your initial $100,000 investment, you've gained a meager $637—not $5,000—in actual purchasing power.

So what does this mean?

So what does all this mean to you? It means you need to start planning now for retirement because you may live longer and need more money than you think, and you may not have as long to work and save for retirement as you expect. Because of the destructive duo of inflation and taxes, it means you will need a sufficient income stream to make sure you don't outlive your retirement income—a very real threat for today's Baby Boomers. One survey showed that 60 percent of U.S. workers said the total value of their savings and investments was less than $25,000.[13]

So the challenge is clear. You need to construct a portfolio that will outperform inflation while taking taxes into account—and develop

---

[13] 2012 Employee Benefit Research Institute's Retirement Confidence Survey.

some sound strategies that will ensure the freedom and lifestyle you envision throughout retirement.

When can I retire?

As people approach retirement, and certainly after they retire, they tend to become more conservative with their investment selections. As a rule of thumb, this makes good sense. But it's important to not become too conservative too early. Why? To answer that question, let's consider a case study involving a married couple named Bill and Reba.

Bill and Reba

Bill and Reba plan to retire in 15 years and do not want to work during retirement. They figure they can live on 80 percent of what they're spending today by cutting back on their expenses during retirement. Multiplying their current monthly expenses of $5,500 by .80 (80 percent) reduces their monthly expenses in retirement to $4,400. But now we need to adjust that $4,400 for inflation. Assuming an inflation rate of 3 percent over the next 15 years, the "inflation factor" is 1.558. When we multiply $4,400 by our inflation factor of 1.558, we get inflation-adjusted expenses of $6,855 a month at retirement. If we multiply those estimated monthly expenses of $6,855 by 12 months, the result is $82,260, which is an estimate of Bill and Reba's inflation-adjusted annual expenses at retirement. That's $16,260 more than their current annual expenses of $66,000.

Now, to make things easy to calculate, let's assume Bill and Reba are the same age, expect to retire at age 65, and anticipate living 20 years in retirement until they die at age 85. Let's also assume the inflation rate is 3 percent over their 20-year retirement. By multiplying their inflation-adjusted annual expenses at retirement ($82,260) by the proper inflation factor, we can predict their annual expenses to climb to $84,728 in Year 1 of retirement. By Year 5 those expenses will increase to $95,339, by Year 10 they will soar to $110,557, and by Year 20 they will rise to $148,562. So Bill and Reba, whose annual living expenses today are $66,000, will have inflation-adjusted expenses totaling $2,276,874 over the course of their 20-year retirement.

To keep things in perspective, we should point out that Bill and Reba will probably not have to save the entire amount of their retirement expenses. Why? Because it's likely they have accumulated savings and investments that should produce a steady stream of income, and will probably receive Social Security payments and possibly pension checks. But we think you get the point. Namely, that you will need a good deal more money than you previously thought to live comfortably in retirement.

How much more money, you ask? Let's take another look at Bill and Reba. They figure they'll need an annual income of $75,000 in today's dollars to live comfortably in retirement, so how much retirement savings do they need today to ensure that $75,000-a-year income? Assuming an average annual yield of 6 percent on their fully invested savings and a 3 percent inflation rate—and also assuming their principle is $0 at the end of their lives—they would need a total of $1,157,642 if they live 20 years in retirement, and $1,530,081 if they live 30 years in retirement.

For most people, that's a lot of money. That's why developing a retirement plan is so crucial, and why a flawed plan can sour the sweetest of retirement dreams. In the next chapter we will look at some of the most common retirement planning mistakes, and how to avoid them.

> "Never test the depth of the water with both feet."
> -Doug Hughes

3

RETIREMENT HURDLES

Though Americans enjoy one of the highest per capita incomes and standards of living in the world, many of them find they are either unable to retire when they'd planned or end up living their retirement years in virtual poverty. Why are their dreams derailed? More often than not, it's because they fail to develop a comprehensive financial plan, making them vulnerable to what we call the 10 retirement roadblocks—forcing them to take costly and often irrevocable detours off the road to financial success.

The Big 10

Here are the 10 major planning roadblocks that can undermine even the best of retirement intentions. In this chapter we will discuss strategies you can use to avoid the first three of these roadblocks. We'll examine how to swerve around the others in later chapters:

- Failing to educate yourself about personal finance, take your financial inventory by tracking your net worth and cash flow.
- Failing to invest early in life or on a regular basis.
- Failing to use tax laws to your advantage.

- Failing to define your lifestyle goals in retirement.
- Failing to establish financial goals designed to help you achieve your lifestyle goals.
- Failing to allocate your assets properly and adjust those allocations as needed.
- Failing to plan for the unexpected.
- Failing to take full advantage of your employer benefit plan and to choose the smartest way to take money out of that plan.
- Failing to properly plan your estate.
- Failing to create a comprehensive financial plan.

Taking financial inventory

Many of us have a vague idea about our financial situation, but in order to reach our retirement goals we need to be specific. The best way to take a snapshot of your current financial status is to create two documents—your *financial statement,* which will show you your net worth; and your *cash flow statement,* which will delineate your income and expenses.

Putting together your financial statement will enable you to see where you are right now, and revising it each year can help you evaluate how well you are progressing toward your retirement goals. Your cash flow statement helps you track how much money came into your household during a certain period of time vs. how much money went out. It can be measured on a monthly basis, or—since some expenses occur only once each year—on an annual basis. A cash flow statement can help you determine how you're spending your money, and how you can better manage your finances to bolster your net worth.

Creating your financial statement

To create your financial statement, the first step is to add up the realistic market value of the things you own, called *assets*. These would include *liquid assets* such as cash, savings accounts, money market funds, and CDs; *investments* such as mutual funds, stocks, bonds and annuities; *retirement accounts* such as 401ks, IRAs and Roth IRAs; *real estate* such as personal residence, vacation home or rental property; and *personal property* such as cars, boats and household items.

The second step involves adding up your debts, called *liabilities*. These would include *consumer debt*, such as credit card debt, car loans and personal loans; *long-term debt* such as real estate mortgages and student loans; and *miscellaneous items* such as current income taxes and loans from life insurance policies. By subtracting your total liabilities from your total assets, you can determine your net worth.

Creating your cash flow statement

To create your cash flow statement, first add up your *total income and earnings*. These would include such things as salary and wages, bonuses and commissions, interest income and rental income. Then add up your *total expenses*. Your total expenses consist of your *savings and investment contributions* into such things as mutual funds, money market accounts, savings accounts, and stocks and bonds; *fixed expenses* such as federal income tax, state and local tax, property tax, and homeowners insurance; and *variable expenses* such as food, gasoline, vacations and medical bills. Finally, subtract your total expenses from your total income and earnings to determine your cash flow.

David Hays and Doug Hughes
Managing credit and debt

Because credit is so pervasive in today's world, many of us have a "buy now, pay later" mentality that can spiral out of control and become a massive retirement roadblock. Credit per se is not problematic, but it must be managed wisely. Some people are convinced that debt is a dirty word, but borrowing money to buy a home, start a business, or get career training is what we call *useful debt* because it can actually brighten your financial picture.

Sometimes we encounter *unavoidable debt* when money is needed to buy a computer for work, pay for medical bills, or purchase a car to get you to and from work. Sometimes, despite your best intentions, life throws you a curve ball—in the form of a lost job, divorce, or disability—that forces you into unavoidable debt.

What you must strive to avoid, with every ounce of your being, is what we call *bad debt*—the kind that we accumulate when we borrow to buy unneeded items such as expensive vacations, fancy furniture, or excessive clothes. Bad debt is truly the Budgetary Boogieman, because it can not only cripple your cash flow, but hinder your ability to obtain credit to buy big-ticket items such as a home.

It can be avoided by pausing before you purchase and asking yourself some candid questions— "Do I really need a new car right now, or could I drive my current model for a couple more years?" "I know a remodeled kitchen with granite countertops would be awesome, but is that something I can put on hold for awhile?" "My family would love a two-week Hawaiian vacation, but is it worth going several thousand dollars in debt?"

ELIMINATING BAD DEBT

But if you find yourself in the bad debt ditch, whether due to poor choices or fate, what can you do to dig yourself out?

- Step 1 is to make sure you understand how you accumulated your bad debt in the first place. If it stemmed from buying too many clothes or eating at too many swanky restaurants, you might want to allot yourself a specified amount of money each month to spend on clothing and restaurants. If you have a penchant for purchasing *toys*—motorboats, jet skis, four-wheelers—you might want to rein in your recreational spending until you eliminate your debt on those items. And we know this sounds a little righteous, but you may even want to sell a few of those toys.
- Step 2 involves such strategies as closing your non-essential accounts; consolidating your debts at a low interest rate; or increasing the payments on your highest-interest debt, and once you've wiped it out, applying those payments to your second-highest interest debt until it disappears.... and so on. If you feel you need professional help, don't hesitate to see a credit counselor.
- Step 3 is optional, and available only to homeowners. It's the acquisition of a home equity loan to pay off your bad debt. A home equity loan is usually available at an interest rate far lower than credit card rates and provides you with interest you can generally deduct on your tax return. But this is a step you should take only after careful consideration. You need to ask yourself if you can afford the added expense of obtaining a mortgage loan, and whether you will be able to make larger mortgage

payments. If you can't, and impulsively obtain this type of loan, you may end up losing your home.
- Step 4, called the maintenance step, should be taken once you're out of debt. It involves paying off your credit cards every month, and if you can't do that, closing those accounts. One thing to keep in mind is that closing an account may result in a lower credit score, because it would result in a higher debt-to-available-credit ratio. Closing an account could result in lower credit score.

CREDIT REPORT

A quick word about your credit report, a tool used by lenders whenever you apply for a car loan, home mortgage or credit card. This report helps lending professionals determine how risky it is to lend you money, and also what interest they will charge you if they decide to grant you a loan or credit card. In the United States there are three major credit reporting agencies—Experian, Equifax, and Trans Union. You are entitled to a free credit report from each of these agencies every year. To order your free credit report, call 877-322-8228 or visit www.annualcreditreport.com.

Invest early and regularly

One of the most common retirement roadblocks is the failure of people to begin investing for retirement early enough and to continue investing on a regular basis. The earlier you invest the better because it gives you more years to allow the power of compound interest to work in your favor, but it's never too late to get started. Not long ago, I (Doug) had six people in their 90s come see me during a two-week span, asking about investment opportunities. Clearly, they didn't think they were too old to make sure their money was working for them. You shouldn't think that either, regardless of your age.

THE POWER OF COMPOUND INTEREST

To help you understand the power of compound interest, think of the oft-quoted maxim—*time is money*. Compound interest uses the combination of time and the reinvestment of interest and sometimes dividends to make your investment grow exponentially.

If you made an initial investment of $50,000 and added $1,000 monthly contributions to that investment for 10 years—and you earned a modest 4 percent on that money—you would end up with $221,791. That's not bad, but if you earned 10 percent you would have $340,197 after 10 years. What if you made the same $50,000 initial investment and $1,000 monthly contributions over 20 years? At 4 percent interest, you would wind up with $477,904. At 10 percent interest you would have the tidy sum of $1,125,773. Now let's stretch that same $50,000 initial investment and $1,000 monthly contributions over 30 years. At 4 percent interest you would end up with $859,724, and at 10 percent interest you would have $3,252,358. For most of us, $3.2 million would finance even the wildest of our retirement dreams.

Using taxes to your advantage

Another common retirement roadblock is failing to use tax laws to your advantage. Most wealthy people know ways to legally pay fewer taxes, resulting in more dollars in their pockets. But those same strategies are available to those with more modest wealth. We want to present you with some strategies that can save you money on your tax return this year, with the caveat that before you implement any of these strategies you should make sure it complements your overall financial plan.

Every situation is unique, and things like *phase outs* and the *alternative minimum tax* might make some of these strategies ineffective or even counter-productive. Phase outs refer to provisions in the tax code that are phased out, meaning their value is gradually reduced as a person's income increases. The alternative minimum tax is an income tax imposed at a nearly flat rate on an adjusted amount of taxable income above a certain threshold that is substantially higher than the threshold associated with regular income tax.

PARTICIPATE IN YOUR EMPLOYER-SPONSORED RETIREMENT PLAN

In most employer-sponsored retirement plans, such as a 401k, you don't pay any taxes on your contributions, which saves you money by reducing the amount of your *taxable income*—your income after subtracting adjustments, exemptions and standard or itemized deductions. These plans also provide you with long-term tax benefits because your principal and earnings grow tax-deferred until they're withdrawn.

CONTRIBUTE TO A TRADITIONAL IRA

If your company does not offer you an employer-sponsored retirement plan, consider making contributions to a traditional IRA. You can contribute up to the lesser of a specified dollar amount that changes every year (or an even higher amount if you're over age 50) or 100 percent of your annual earned income. Consult your financial advisor for the current figures. Depending on your income, you may be able to deduct your contributions. A traditional IRA, like a 401k, also gives you the long-term benefit of tax-deferred growth.

CONTRIBUTE TO FLEXIBLE SPENDING ACCOUNTS

Flexible spending accounts are sometimes provided by employers to enable their employees to set aside pre-tax dollars from their paychecks for qualified dependent or health care expenses throughout the year. Using such an account will reduce your taxable income, but you have to plan carefully because funds in some types of these accounts must be forfeited if they are not used before the end of the year.

CONSIDER TAX IMPLICATIONS BEFORE YOU RETIRE

Because your final paycheck from your company may be your largest, it might be to your advantage to retire at the beginning of the calendar year—a year in which your taxable income may be less than the previous year.

ITEMIZE TAX DEDUCTIONS

On your tax return you can take a *standard deduction* from your taxable income. You don't need any records to prove you deserve this deduction because it's given to anyone who wants to take it. The amount of the deduction is based on your filing status. There are standard deductions for a single or married person filing separately, for a married couple filing jointly or a qualifying widower, and for a head of household. These deductions changes yearly, so consult your financial advisor for the latest figures.

If your qualifying expenses exceed your standard deduction you can reduce your taxable income by itemizing your deductions, though for some higher income taxpayers itemized deductions are partially phased out. If you choose to itemize your deductions—things like state and local income taxes, property taxes, charitable donations, unreimbursed business expenses, mortgage interest paid, and medical and dental expenses above a certain percentage of your adjusted gross income—you must maintain records of every expenditure you itemize. If you're audited by the Internal Revenue Service, you will have to produce those records.

CONSOLIDATE DEDUCTIBLE EXPENSES

If you don't have enough deductions to make it worth your while to itemize each year, you might want to make some slight modifications to when you pay for certain deductible expenses—enabling you to maximize your savings by itemizing deductions one year and taking the standard deduction the following year. For example, you can have all your non-essential medical or dental work performed in the same calendar year, or make all your charitable contributions in the same calendar year by giving next year's contribution at the end of this year. Other consolidation strategies are selling depreciated securities to take the loss as a tax deduction, then donating the cash from the sale to charity; prepaying your estimated state income tax balance instead of waiting until next April; prepaying the second installment of your property tax (assuming you are not subject to the alternative minimum tax), and making your January mortgage payment the prior year (sending in your payment well in advance so it will be reflected on the 1098 form sent to the IRS). You can also donate appreciated long-term securities to get a full fair market value deduction without paying any tax on your *capital gains*—increases in the value of a capital asset that gives it a higher value than the purchase price. (A capital gain is not realized until you sell the asset. Realized gains for assets held 12 or fewer months are taxed at the same rate as ordinary income, but assets held for more than 12 months are normally taxed at a lower rate. In most cases, you can exclude any capital gains—up to a specified dollar figure on an individual tax return and a larger figure on a joint return—resulting from the sale of your primary residence. Consult your financial advisor for the latest caps).

TAKE ADVANTAGE OF ADJUSTMENTS AND TAX CREDITS

Using *adjustments* and *tax credits* are two strategies that are commonly overlooked, but each can put cash in your pocket when making your tax calculations. Adjustments include such things as alimony paid, moving expenses, interest paid on student loans, and eligible contributions to a traditional IRA.

Adjustments are certainly worth claiming because they are deducted from your taxable income before subtracting any deductions, credits, or *exemptions*. Exemptions allow you to reduce your taxable income for yourself, your spouse, and each of your dependent children. Adjustments might also allow you to qualify for certain types of tax deductions that are based on a percentage of your *adjusted gross income*—your gross income minus certain specified expenses. Your AGI is the amount from which standard or itemized deductions and personal and dependent exemptions are deducted to determine the amount that you will be taxed.

Tax credits are actually more valuable than deductions because unlike deductions—which reduce only the amount of income that is taxed—tax credits provide a dollar-for-dollar reduction of your federal income tax for qualifying investments or for payments you made for such things as education, child and dependent care, foreign taxes, or an adoption. The American Opportunity Credit provides an annual tax credit up to $2,500 per student, and the Lifetime Learning Credit offers a tax credit of 20 percent of your qualified educational expenses up to $10,000. Some states, like our home State of Indiana, offer tax credits for contributing to a 529 College Savings Plan.

USE CAPITAL LOSS RULES TO YOUR ADVANTAGE

Capital losses—securities sold for less than what you paid for them—can be used to offset any capital gains you might have as long as those securities are in a taxable account. If your capital losses exceed your capital gains during the tax year, you can use up to $3,000 ($1,500 for each married person filing separately) of those losses to shrink your earned income, thus reducing your taxable income. Any losses above $3,000 can be carried forward to offset gains in future years with no expiration date. But be careful. The Wash Sale Rule says if you sell a security at a loss and buy back the same security within 30 days of the sale, that loss is not allowed for income tax purposes. If you don't want your money to be out of the market for a full month, you might consider finding a similar-but-different investment— usually in the same asset class—to replace the security you sold.

BE SMART ABOUT MUTUAL FUNDS

When it comes to buying and selling mutual funds in a manner that maximizes your tax advantages, timing is everything. By purchasing a mutual fund after the annual distribution of capital gains and dividends, you can avoid paying taxes on that distribution. You might also consider selling mutual funds that are expected to pay a large dividend before the *record date*—the date by which you must own shares to receive declared dividends or capital gains distributions. In some cases, selling mutual funds might allow you to pay capital gains rates instead of ordinary income tax rates (which are higher than capital gains rates) on non-qualifying dividends.

PUT ASSETS IN DIFFERENT TYPES OF ACCOUNTS

If you are able to save more money for retirement than you are allowed to contribute to tax-deferred accounts, consider putting your more tax-efficient investments (things like Exchange Traded Funds, Real Estate Investment Trust funds and tax-free bonds) in taxable accounts and your less tax-efficient investments (such as mutual funds and stocks) in tax-deferred accounts.

CONSIDER BUYING INVESTMENTS WITH TAX ADVANTAGES

There are five main types of investments that offer you tax advantages:

- Tax-deferred investments—such as 401 (k), 403 (b), and 457 plans; IRAs; variable annuities; and fixed annuities. These investments allow you to invest before-tax or after-tax dollars and delay paying taxes on contributions and earnings until you withdraw them. The money withdrawn is usually taxed as ordinary income, though it may be subject to tax penalties.
- Tax-deductible investments —such as 401(k), 403(b), and 457 plans; and IRAs. These investments allow you to invest before-tax dollars or after-tax dollars, thus enabling you to lower your current taxable income. The money you withdraw is usually taxed as ordinary income, though it may be subject to tax penalties.

- Tax-exempt investments, such as municipal bonds. This type of investment allows you to invest after-tax dollars, and the interest income you earn from the investment is normally not subject to federal or state income taxes. It's only exempt from state and local taxes if you buy bonds issued by the state or city in which you live. Municipal bonds are also subject to the alternative minimum tax.
- Tax-free investments, such as Roth IRAs and life insurance. These investments allow you to invest after-tax dollars, and no taxes will be owed when you withdraw the money. Distributions under the life insurance policy—including cash, *dividends*, and partial or full *surrenders*—are not subject to taxation up to the amount paid into the policy. A dividend is a distribution of a portion of a company's earnings to a class of its shareholders, and is often quoted as the dollar each share receives (qualified dividends are taxed at a lower rate than ordinary income). A partial surrender is the removal of a portion of the original cash balance of an insurance policy, which result in a fee and a reduction in the policy's value. A full surrender is the distribution of the entire original investment account of an insurance policy, which may result in a fee and the termination of the policy.
- Tax credits, such as the American Opportunity Credit or credits received from low-income housing. These tax credits can be used to offset your taxes due—dollar for dollar.

> "The secret to a happy retirement is faith, family, friends…. and a fixed income stream!"
> -David Hays

4

AVAILABLE INCOME SOURCES

Many of us rely on three primary sources of retirement income—Social Security; employer-sponsored retirement plans; and personal retirement sources such as IRAs and Roth IRAs. In this chapter, we'll learn how to maximize the income stream from each of these sources by qualifying for tax deductions, deferring taxes, and avoiding penalties; and how to remain financially flexible after retirement so we can adjust to the inevitable curve balls life tends to throw our way. We'll also take a look at the current eligibility and benefit rules for Social Security, and changes that might be coming to the program in the years ahead.

Perhaps the most common *personal retirement sources* are Individual Retirement Accounts, commonly referred to as IRAs. An IRA is not actually an investment per se, but an investment plan—one designed to provide you with federal income tax benefits on retirement investments such as money markets, stocks and mutual funds within a retirement account. Because IRAs provide you with virtually unlimited investment choices, they offer you tremendous flexibility when planning your retirement income strategy. There are two major types of IRAs—traditional IRAs and Roth IRAs.

Traditional IRAs

People often have traditional IRAs if they are not participating in an *employer-sponsored qualified retirement plan* (a qualified plan is one that's available to all company employees), are already making maximum contributions to their employer's plan, or want to transfer money from their employer's plan to an IRA due to retirement or a job change. Some spouses with no earned income, such as stay-at-home moms, like to use a traditional IRA to accumulate assets for retirement. A traditional IRA allows your money to grow *tax-deferred*, meaning you defer paying taxes on earnings within your IRA account until you withdraw them—presumably when you're retired and in a lower federal income tax bracket. You can generally make penalty-free withdrawals after age 59½, but later in this chapter we'll show you a few ways you can get money out of your traditional IRA before 59½ without incurring any penalties.

PARTICIPATION RULES AND CONTRIBUTION LIMITS

Traditional IRAs have participation rules and contribution limits. To contribute money, you must be under age 70½ and have *earned income*. What's earned income? Think, "May I take your order?" or "Welcome to Walmart." Simply put, it's money you earn at a job. You can contribute any amount up to 100 percent of your earned income as long as it does not exceed a set amount (or a higher amount if you're over age 50). Married couples can contribute up to twice the individual amount per year provided at least one of them has earned income. Non-working spouses are exempted from the earned income requirement, and can contribute a set amount per year. It's a good idea to consult with a qualified financial advisor to learn the various amounts, which can change from year to year.

One nice thing about a traditional IRA, particularly for those who enjoy immediate gratification, is that it gives you a tax deduction this year. And any contributions you make up to April 15 of the current year will still count for the previous year. If you're working a part-time job for the sole purpose of accumulating future retirement income and are making less than the allowable amount or less a year, you can put all your earnings into a traditional IRA and not pay a penny's worth of taxes on those earnings until you withdraw them in retirement.

THE POWER OF TAX-DEFERRED GROWTH

To see the power of tax-deferred growth provided by a traditional IRA, let's compare two investment accounts—a non-IRA or taxable account in which you pay the taxes up front and a traditional IRA in which you defer paying taxes until you withdraw the money.

Consider John, who makes an initial investment of $5,500, plus $5,500 per year over 15 years in a taxable account. We'll assume his income places him in a tax bracket of 25 percent, so his net, after-tax contribution each year would be $4,125. We'll also assume a 15 percent tax rate on his investments (qualified dividends and capital gains) in that taxable account, and—assuming a pre-tax return of 8 percent—a net after-tax return of 6.8 percent. After 15 years, he would have a balance of $113,140.

But if John were to make that same initial investment of $5,500, plus $5,500 per year over 15 years in a traditional IRA, he would get a $5,500 tax deduction each year, and that money would grow tax-free for 15 years—mushrooming to $166,784. At the end of 15 years, he would have to pay $41,696 in taxes if he withdrew the money, but his IRA account balance would still be $125,088, substantially higher than the $113,140 he'd have if his money had been in a taxable account. But because the odds of John withdrawing all his IRA money out at one time are slim to none, his IRA nest egg will continue to grow at an impressive rate beyond the 15-year period. More than likely, he would withdraw the money in small increments—paying taxes on those incremental withdrawals while allowing the account balance to continue growing.

TAX DEDUCTIBILITY OF CONTRIBUTIONS

Generally, 100 percent of your traditional IRA contribution is tax deductible unless you're an *active* participant in an employer-sponsored retirement plan and your adjusted gross income is more than a specified amount. Even if you are not participating in the plan, you are still considered *active* if you are eligible to participate in the plan. The tax-deductibility phase-outs vary according to your filing status, your adjusted gross income, and whether you're an active participant in an employer-sponsored plan.

If you are a single person or head of household who's covered by a retirement plan at work, you can still qualify for a full traditional IRA deduction if your adjusted gross income is below a specified amount, which changes each year. If your adjusted gross income is within a specified range higher than that, you can qualify for a partial deduction, and if your AGI is larger than a certain amount you can't qualify for any deduction.

If you're married, filing jointly, or a qualifying widow or widower who's covered by a retirement plan at work, you can still qualify for a full traditional IRA deduction if your adjusted gross income is below a specified figure, but if your AGI falls within a specified range higher than that you are eligible for just a partial deduction. If your AGI is beyond a certain figure, you can't qualify for any deduction at all. The set figures can change from year to year.

If you're married, filing separately, and covered by a retirement plan at work, you can't qualify for a full traditional IRA deduction, regardless of your income. But you can qualify for a partial deduction if your AGI is below a certain set amount. Consult a qualified financial consultant to learn what the income limits are for the current year.

But what if you are *not* eligible for a retirement plan at work? If you're a single person or head of household, you can get a full traditional IRA deduction regardless of your AGI. If you're married, filing separately, you can't qualify for a full deduction if your AGI is more than a specified amount, but you can qualify for a partial deduction if your income is below that figure.

If you're a married couple, filing jointly, it's a little more complicated. If both of you are covered by an employer plan, you can't deduct an IRA contribution unless you as a couple earn less than the phase-out amounts. If one of you is covered by an employer plan and the other is not, then the spouse who is not covered by a plan can make fully deductible contribution to a traditional IRA.

DISTRIBUTION RULES, TAXES AND PENALTIES

Penalty-free withdrawals from traditional IRAs can begin after age 59½. I (David) can still remember hearing the unbridled excitement in my Dad's voice when he phoned me the day he turned 59½ and said, "Son, I just had an Aha moment! I realized that as of today I can take money from my retirement account without paying a penalty!"

But even if you're old enough to make penalty-free withdrawals, that doesn't mean you can elude the inescapable Tax Man. You must pay taxes on the deductible contributions and earnings when you take withdrawals from your traditional IRA account. Sure, it's a smart move to defer paying taxes over a long period of time, but there is a mortgage on that money, and that mortgage is, in essence, the taxes that ultimately must be paid. So just as you have to pay off a home mortgage before you own your home free-and-clear, you have to eventually pay off the mortgage on your IRA before it becomes a free-and-clear asset.

As we said earlier, prior to reaching that 59½-year milestone, you may have to pay a 10 percent penalty on the amount withdrawn from your traditional IRA. But there are a few exceptions. Withdrawals from your IRA can be made penalty-free if they are used for qualified education expenses for yourself or your children, first-time home-buying expenses up to a set lifetime maximum, qualified medical expenses, disability or death. Qualified medical expenses are medical expenses that are necessary to maintain your health, not things like eyebrow lifts or tummy tucks. And death gets you out of just about everything, including paying penalties on early IRA withdrawals made by your beneficiaries.

Penalties can also be avoided if distributions are made to you in a series of substantially equal payments. Let's say you are 58 years old and need to withdraw some money from your IRA for a reason that does not qualify for a penalty-exemption. If you take a series of equal withdrawals from that account and pay the taxes on each withdrawal, you will not have to pay any penalty to the IRS.

If you have a traditional IRA, you must begin taking *required minimum distributions* (withdrawals or RMD's) from your account prior to April

1 of the year after you turn 70½ and every year thereafter. This is the IRS's way of saying, "It's time to start paying the tax". However if you wait until April 1st of the year after you turn 70 ½ to take your first distribution, you will have to take two in that year, your 70 ½ and 71 distributions. The only time you would consider delaying your distribution is if your taxable income is going to be less in the year following your 70 ½ "birthday". There is only one exception to taking RMD's — if you are still working and are an *active* participant in an employer-sponsored plan, you can delay taking a required minimum distributions from that plan until you stop working. Many of our clients are in their 70s and still working, often part-time. They frequently choose to take advantage of this exception to preserve the strength of their IRA account.

If you don't take your required minimum distribution —if you withdraw nothing or not enough from the account—you will incur a tax penalty equal to 50 percent of the difference between the required distribution and the actual distribution! That will sting enough to raise a good-sized welt on your psyche. If your minimum distribution is $10,000, for example, and you mistakenly take out only $5,000, your penalty would be half of $5,000—or $2,500.

Roth IRAs

We like to use farmer language to explain Roth IRAs. When you open a Roth IRA account, you are paying taxes on the seed, but you won't pay taxes on the harvest. Most farmers would leap at that opportunity in a heartbeat, and that's why you should strongly consider the Roth, in which you pay taxes on the money up front, but not on the back side when you take the money out.

Your contributions and earnings compound tax-deferred, and after age 59½—as long as you've had your money in a Roth for at least five years—you can withdraw your contributions and earnings tax-free. If you withdraw money from a Roth before the five-year holding period has expired, you will pay taxes and penalties on that account's growth, but not on your contributions, because you would have already paid taxes on those contributions.

Roth IRAs are particularly attractive to people who feel their tax rate might actually be higher during retirement than it is now, are unable to deduct contributions to a traditional IRA, or want to keep making contributions to their Roth IRA as long they're still earning income—even after 70½. The IRS allows you to make Roth contributions after 70½ as long as you still have earned income. I (David) have a 76-year-old client who runs an apple orchard. He loves his work so much that he plans to keep operating that orchard until he's 90, and to continue making annual contributions to his Roth until he finally retires. Another reason to consider a Roth is if you're close to retiring and don't want to start taking minimum distributions by age 70½. Unlike a traditional IRA, you are not required to start taking minimum withdrawals from a Roth IRA by age 70½.

We feel Roth IRAs should be part of most people's portfolios, because they provide tax-status diversification, something that is every bit as important to your retirement strategy as investment diversification. If you have a mixture of Roth IRAs and traditional IRAs, you'll pay taxes on some accounts when you pull the money out, but pay no taxes when you take money out of other accounts. This healthy balance will allow you to strategically withdraw money from the right account at the right time, reducing the taxes you pay in the process.

ROTH IRA PARTICIPATION RULES AND CONTRIBUTION LIMITS

Though Roth IRA contributions must be made with after-tax dollars, the same contribution limits that apply to a traditional IRA apply to a Roth—meaning you can contribute up to 100 percent of your annual earned income or a set amount per year (a higher amount if you're over age 50), whichever is less. The annual contribution limit for a non-working spouse is a set figure, and the contribution limit for a married couple is higher if at least one spouse has earned income. And just as with traditional IRAs, Roth IRA contributions can be made as late as April 15 for the prior year.

But there are some income limitations for Roth IRA contributions. If your adjusted gross income is above a specified amount, your annual maximum contribution limit is incrementally reduced. A single person or a married couple filing jointly can make a full contribution, partial contribution, or no contribution—depending on the amount of their adjusted gross income. Married couples filing separately cannot make a full contribution, but they can make a partial contribution if their adjusted gross income is below a set figure. Consult an experienced financial advisor for the current limits.

CONVERTING TO A ROTH IRA

You are allowed by law to convert some or all of your traditional IRA to a Roth IRA, regardless of your income. Let's say you have $100,000 in a traditional IRA and want to convert that to a Roth. You will have to pay income taxes up front on that money at your current tax rate, and that might sting a little. But in return, you will be able to make tax-free withdrawals—and be free from required minimum distributions—throughout retirement.

Converting a traditional IRA to a Roth IRA is an excellent way to take advantage of the lower tax rates recently implemented by the Tax Cuts and Jobs Act of 2017. For example, if your annual taxable income for married filing a joint return is between $19,051 and $77,400, the new law lowers your tax rate on that income from 15 to 12 percent, the 10 percent bracket stayed the same. If your annual taxable income falls between $77,401 and $165,000, your tax rate on that income has been lowered from 25 to 22 percent. If your annual taxable income is between $165,001 and $315,000, your tax rate on that amount has been cut from 28 to 24 percent. All of these taxable income ranges are after you take your standard deduction of $24,000 and a $1,300 exemption for each of you are over age 65.

In 2008 and 2009, when the stock market plunged about 50 percent, we helped scores of our clients do Roth IRA conversions, and they're all smiling today. When the stock market rebounded, and their Roth accounts rose with it like ships at high tide, their bountiful earnings were tax-free.

One thing to keep in mind is that if you're converting a traditional IRA that's been funded with tax-deductible contributions, you will have to pay taxes on your contributions and earnings; but if you're converting a traditional IRA that's been funded with non-deductible contributions (you can make non-deductible contributions into a traditional IRA regardless of your income as long as you have earned income), you will have to pay taxes only on your earnings.

Funding traditional IRAs with non-deductible contributions was popular in the 1980s and early 1990s, and some of those accounts are quite sizeable by now. If you have one of these accounts and want to convert it to a Roth IRA, you will not have to again pay taxes on that money—called your *basis*—because you've already paid taxes on it. But here's something you need to know. It's up to you to keep track of your basis, and there is a tax form—Form 8606—that will help you do that. You simply fill out the form and file it with the IRS to establish your basis.

Over the years, we've seen a number of people get burned by forgetting to tell their tax preparer they didn't take any tax deductions when they put money into their traditional IRA, so when they converted the account to a Roth—or when they simply withdrew the money to spend—they paid taxes on it a second time.

People who inherit a retirement account almost always overlook this. That's why, if you inherit a traditional IRA, the first question you should ask is, "Is there a basis in this account?" If the answer is yes, then you don't have to pay taxes on that basis.

Another often overlooked aspect of Roth IRA conversions is that you don't have to convert all of your IRA at once. If you do it in stages over the course of many years—as opposed to converting in a single year—you can often pay a significantly smaller amount of total tax. Let's assume you have $100,000 in a traditional retirement account that you want to convert to a Roth IRA, but if you convert it all it would cost you too much money, consider converting smaller amounts each year. Let's say you are in the 15% tax bracket and you could have $15,000 more income and still only pay 15%. You could convert $15,000 to a Roth one year, another $15,000 the next year.... and so on. That way, you can incrementally convert all of your taxable dollars to tax-free dollars, and do it painlessly. If you don't use up your tax bracket, it's like not using a gift card that expires at the end of each year.

But you need to be wary of a potential pitfall. Remember how we said that if you're converting a traditional IRA that's been funded with tax-deductible contributions to a Roth IRA that you will have to pay taxes on both your contributions and earnings? Well, you should try to pay those taxes with funds other than your IRA funds. Let's say you are under 59 ½ and have a $100,000 balance in your traditional IRA and you owe a $25,000 tax on that amount for converting it to a Roth. If you use other funds to pay that $25,000 tax, your Roth IRA balance will remain at $100,000. But if you tap into your IRA funds to pay the $25,000 tax, you will have to take $25,000 out of your IRA, pay a $2,857 early-withdrawal penalty, and pay a $714 tax on the penalty—leaving your IRA with only $71,429.

ELIMINATION OF THE ROTH CONVERSION DO-OVER

Beginning Jan. 1, 2017, due to the Tax Cuts and Jobs Act of 2017, you can no longer do a Roth conversion *recharacterization*, which was essentially a do-over. Recharacterization had been allowed through a provision in the law that permitted you—after converting a traditional IRA to a Roth IRA—to recharacterize it back to a traditional IRA, provided you did it by Oct. 15 of the following year.

This provision has been eliminated.

ROTH IRA BACK DOOR METHOD

Remember when we talked about the income limitations for Roth IRA contributions? Well, if your adjusted gross income is too high to make a partial or full Roth IRA contribution, you can get around that pesky problem by using what we call the *back door method*. This simply involves making a non-deductible contribution into a traditional IRA (you can make non-deductible contributions into a traditional IRA regardless of your income), then immediately converting it to a Roth IRA. Because you received no deduction from your original contribution, there is no tax on that contribution when you convert. The backdoor method is widely used by financial professionals and tax strategists, but if you want to use this strategy you would be wise to do it sooner rather than later. We feel it's only a matter of time before the IRS closes this loophole in the law.

ROTH IRA DISTRIBUTION RULES, TAXES AND PENALTIES

In general, there are no required minimum distributions from a Roth IRA account during your entire lifetime. The only exception occurs if you inherit a Roth IRA, in which case you have to take minimum distributions, but those distributions are still not taxable. If you fail to take a minimum distribution from an inherited Roth IRA by the end of the year following the account holder's death, you'll have to pay a tax penalty equal to 50 percent of the difference between the required distribution and the actual distribution.

Contributions must be in your Roth IRA for at least five years before you can begin taking qualified distributions at age 59½ free of taxes and penalties. If you don't meet the holding period, you will have to pay penalties and taxes. If you have one or more Roth IRA accounts, the five-year holding period starts at the beginning of the year in which you first set up a Roth IRA account (the holding period for an inherited Roth IRA is determined independently of any other Roth IRA you own).

Let's say in 2010 you open a Roth IRA and put $2,000 into it, then contribute $3,000 more in 2011 and $4,000 more in 2012. In 2015 you could begin taking penalty-free distributions from your Roth because you started it five years prior.

If you've satisfied the holding period for your Roth IRA, you can also make a withdrawal from the account without paying income tax or penalties if the withdrawal is needed prior to age 59½ because of death, disability, or a first-time home purchase up to $10,000. You will pay taxes on the earnings but not incur any penalties if you satisfy the holding period and withdraw from the account to pay for qualified medical expenses, qualified higher education expenses or a series of substantially equal payments over your lifetime.

You must keep any amount of money you've *converted* to a Roth IRA in that Roth account for at least five years and until age 59½ before the money can be withdrawn without penalty. If you fail meet that five-year holding period for a converted account, you'll have to pay a 10 percent penalty on your earnings. The reason you pay a penalty on just your earnings (the harvest) is that you have already paid taxes on your original contribution (the seed).

Other personal retirement income sources

So far we've looked at traditional and Roth IRAs, and later in this chapter we'll discuss Social Security and employer-sponsored retirement plans. But first we want to talk about some other personal retirement income sources, namely:

INVESTMENTS

Investments held outside of your retirement plan—things like annuities, bonds, mutual funds, or certificates of deposit—can provide an important source of retirement income. As you approach retirement, your financial circumstances may change, so you should consider making adjustments to your investment plan that reflect those changes.

EMPLOYMENT INCOME

An estimated 40 percent of boomers are now working in retirement, either because they feel they need the income or because they want to keep their minds sharp and stay engaged with society. Many of our clients retire at 62 or 63, but pick up a part-time job to create some extra income until they reach their full retirement age. Others simply want to dip their toes into the sea of change. I (David) know a woman who retired from a high-stress job with AT&T after working there for 32 years. Now she has a part-time job with at the American Legion, waiting tables and loving every minute of it. The job puts a little cash in her purse, but more importantly, it gives her the interaction with others that she missed. But we'd like to issue a word of caution. You need to crunch the numbers before leaping into the job market, because employment income could possibly reduce your Social Security benefit (if you are under full retirement age) or create a tax burden when combined with annuity payments from a pension plan. That being said, some of our clients have not been deterred by the additional taxes associated with employment. Paying taxes is a little bit like love: it's better to have loved and lost, than to have never loved at all…It's better to have made it and paid it than to have never made it at all!

David Hays and Doug Hughes

INHERITANCES

When I (David) sit down with a new client, one of the first questions I always ask is, "Are you anticipating a large inheritance?" The reason is obvious. If you have a parent or grandparent who is well off and may leave you with a substantial amount of money, you need to incorporate that possibility into your retirement plan. Most of our clients say, "Yeah, I expect to inherit some money, but I'm not counting on it," and that is a good way to look at it. But by the same token, you shouldn't exclude an expected inheritance from your long-term retirement planning.

The U.S. population is currently experiencing the largest transfer of estate assets in our nation's history—from the children of the depression to today's boomers. But the baby boomers may not do the same for their children. Research shows that boomers are far more interested in leaving values and memories to their children, whereas their parents were more concerned about leaving their offspring with the one thing they grew up without—money.

One night we (the Hays family) were having dinner at our home when Will, my then 12-year-old son, asked, "Dad, when you die will I get all this?" I said, "No, Mom & I are going to spend it all, then burn the house down". He didn't believe me, just like most kids don't believe the popular bumper sticker that says, "I'm spending my children's inheritance." My comment to my son, like the bumper sticker, was meant to be funny. But as is the case with most humor, it also contains a grain of truth.

LIFE INSURANCE

Because certain types of life insurance policies accumulate cash value, you may want to borrow from your policy or withdraw some of the money from your policy to use in retirement. But you should keep in mind that if you borrow money from your policy, the interest you'll have to pay on that loan could seriously deplete the policy's cash value that will be provided to your beneficiary. There are times when it can be advantageous to borrow against your policy, but it must be done the right way. Your financial advisor can show you how to borrow wisely.

RENTAL REAL ESTATE

Rental real estate can be a nice supplement to your retirement income. I (David) have owned a few rental properties over the years that generated some significant ordinary income while allowing me to write off such things as depreciation, mortgage interest, property taxes, and repair costs. But with rental properties, things are not always lollipops and rainbows. Your rental unit can sometimes generate a loss instead of a gain, and you may have to evict irresponsible or deadbeat tenants. Then, when you sell the unit, you will have to pay capital gains tax. Some retirees soften the capital gains blow by selling their rental property on contract to generate a steady flow of retirement income. We know a savvy couple that sold an office building on contract that provided them with all the money they needed during the first 10 years of their retirement. If you like the idea of owning rental property but cringe at the notion of managing it, you might consider investing in a *Real Estate Investment Trust*, which we will discuss in greater detail in Chapter 6.

Social Security

Social Security has been around since 1935, when President Roosevelt signed the Social Security Act into law. Today, Social Security represents the largest portion of most Americans' retirement income. For the average American today age 65 or older, nearly 40 percent of his (or her) total retirement income comes from Social Security—with 25 percent coming from earnings, 20 percent from pensions and annuities, 13 percent from other assets, and 2 percent coming from miscellaneous sources.[14] We believe most people should not be relying on Social Security for 40 percent of their retirement income because Social Security's cost of living adjustments tend to be relatively modest, averaging about 2.8 percent per year.

Social Security is funded by payroll taxes received from employers and their employees. If you are self-employed, you must pay both the employer and employee portions of the payroll tax. The monthly income you receive from Social Security is based on your age when you begin receiving benefits and your *historical earnings* (your earnings over the course of your lifetime). Some people think if they're making good money now and work just a couple more years at their current salary, it will significantly boost their Social Security benefits upon retirement. After all, if you work a couple extra years and your employer bases your pension on your average salary over your final five years, those extra years will make your pension checks considerably larger. But that's not how it works with Social Security, because the government factors inflation into the benefit calculation. If, for example, you made $30,000 in 1970, the government will adjust that figure for inflation, converting the $30,000 into today's dollars. What that means is a salary of $60,000

---

[14] Employee Benefit Research Institute

Today's Guide to Retirement Planning

in 2013 may not increase your Social Security benefit any more than a $30,000 salary in 1970 would.

Your full Social Security retirement benefits begin at your *full retirement age*, which is somewhere between 65 and 67 depending on your date of birth. For those born between 1943 and 1964, the full retirement age is 66 years. For those born in 1955, it's 66 years and 2 months. For those born in 1956, it's 66 years and 4 months. For those born in 1960 or later, it's 67 years.

But you can start taking *reduced retirement benefits*—benefits that range from 70 to 80 percent of your full benefit depending on when you begin taking them—as early as age 62. If you were born between 1943 and 1954 and opt for a reduced retirement benefit at age 62, you will receive 75 percent of your full retirement benefit. If you were born in 1958 and begin taking a reduced benefit at 62, your benefit would be 71.67 percent of your full benefit. If you were born in 1960 or later and decide to take a reduced benefit at 62, your benefit would be 70 percent of your full benefit.

A lot of people today, worried about the long-term solvency of Social Security, begin taking reduced benefits at age 62. In fact, one report shows that 41 percent of men and 46 percent of women retire at age 62 for the smallest possible benefit check. [15] We generally advise against doing that. If at all possible, wait at least until your full retirement age to begin taking Social Security benefits. Each year after age 62, your benefit will rise about 8 percent (plus annual *cost-of-living adjustments* based on inflation) until you reach age 70, at which point your annual increase will stop. Think about what that means. Let's say your average

---

[15] 2012 Social Security Administration report.

cost-of-living benefit increases of 3 percent a year. If Social Security increases that by 8 percent per year, it amounts to an 11 percent benefit increase for every year you delay taking benefits until age 70. That's why, if you start taking your benefit at age 70 rather than 66, you could easily beef up your benefit by 40 percent per year.

SOCIAL SECURITY CLAIMING STRATEGIES

When developing your individual claiming strategy, you should carefully consider a number of factors that could significantly affect the amount of your monthly Social Security benefit. These factors include your age, past earnings, future earnings, spousal earnings, pension income, current marital status, previous marital status, widow/widower status, and whether or not you are disabled. Remember, once you claim your Social Security benefit, you have 12 months to change your mind and pay it back, or it is "locked in." Most years your monthly check will increase a few dollars through a Cost of Living Adjustment designed to help your benefit keep pace (somewhat) with inflation.

Though the era of so-called *aggressive* Social Security claiming strategies came to an end in November of 2015, you may still be able to make some tactical moves depending on your specific situation and individual circumstances. For example, you can still use a "file but restrict" strategy if you were 62 as of Jan. 1, 2016. This restricted application allows you to file on someone else's earnings record while delaying your own.

To see how this strategy can work to your advantage, let's assume Mary's full benefit would have been $2,000 a month, but because she begins taking it at age 64 it drops to $1,600 per month. When Mike does a "file and restrict," he begins receiving $1,000 a month—half of what Mary's full benefit would have been. But by delaying his own benefit, which would have been $2,800 at his full retirement age, Mike receives nearly $4,000 a month when he switches to his own benefit at age 70 (which is when his benefit will no longer increase). If Mike should die first, Mary would step up to Mike's benefit. By employing this strategy, many couples can increase their monthly benefit by several thousands more.

There are other ways to use this method. If you were married at least two years and widowed, you can "file and restrict" as early as age 60 and delay your own benefits for 10 years. If you've been married at least 10 years and then get divorced, and didn't remarried before starting Social Security, you can file and restrict to your ex-spouses benefit. You are divorcing your spouse, not the benefits!

It's important to realize that the Social Security Administration will not notify you when you can begin claiming your benefit. It's your responsibility to know what benefit you're entitled to and when you can begin receiving it.

- Social Security benefits are based on your income during your 35 highest-earning years, even if you have worked and put money into the system for more than 35 years.
- You can begin taking reduced benefits at age 62, but you can start receiving full benefits between the ages of 65 and 67, depending on your year of birth.
- If you wait until you are 70 to begin your benefits, you will receive the *maximum* benefit possible. There is no reason to delay claiming Social Security beyond age 70 because benefits stop increasing after that age.

Regardless of when you turn your benefit spigot on, you should consider signing up for Medicare when you become eligible at age 65, because your Medicare premium may cost more (for the rest of your life) if you decline to sign up at 65. Because of recent changes to Medicare, and the expectation of more changes in the future, we strongly recommend using a trusted financial advisor to help you with this process.

One thing to keep in mind is that you can take only one Social Security benefit, so deciding what you take and when you take it is incredibly important. Because this is a decision that has life-long ramifications, and because employees in Social Security field offices are often unaware of all the available claiming strategies, we recommend using a knowledgeable investment advisor to help you through this process.

Social Security office employees will often tell people that whether they begin taking benefits at age 62; at full retirement age (between age 65 and 67); or age 70; they will receive the same total amount of money over the course of their remaining years. But it's very unlikely that this will be the case for you. Unless you anticipate a short lifespan, deciding to begin taking your benefits at age 62 (or even full retirement age) might be the wrong decision–resulting in significantly lower lifetime benefits. Even online benefits calculators can lead you astray. These calculators can spit out incorrect numbers due to missing information, inaccurate data, or "built-in" assumptions (such as underestimating your future earnings) that can result in miscalculations.

We have found that the vast majority of workers begin taking their Social Security benefits too early. Many of them later regret their decision, especially when they realize how much larger their monthly benefits (and lifetime benefits) could have been had they delayed taking their benefits a few years. If you begin receiving your benefits at age 62, you will incur a 25-to-30 percent penalty, and be penalized for any income you generate above a certain threshold, which changes every year. But each year you delay claiming benefits after reaching your full retirement age, your monthly check will grow by 8 percent. If you wait until 70 to start taking your benefit, your monthly check will be a whopping 76 percent larger than it would have been had you begun claiming your benefit at age 62.

The number one push back we hear when we suggest a delay strategy is, "At what age do I break-even?" According to Transamerica, here is how it sorts out. If you take Social Security at 62 rather than 66, your break-even age is 78 (which means you would have been better off waiting). If you take it at 66 rather than 70, your break-even age is 82.5 years. Regardless of which age you take your benefit, in all the years we've been practicing, we've never heard someone who's dying at age 80 say, "Man, I sure wish I would have taken my Social Security earlier!"

Because of these numbers, we recommend that healthy people begin taking benefits as close to age 70 as possible. To make that recommendation a reality, you might consider keeping your current job, finding a second job, or cutting your spending. You might even think about moving to an area with a lower cost of living or simply use more of your nest egg early and use less of it later.

Another thing to keep in mind is that the Windfall Benefit Provision may reduce your Social Security benefit if you also earned a pension from an employer who did not withhold Social Security taxes from your paycheck. Social Security's benefit calculation pays a higher percentage to retired workers with lower Social Security-covered earnings. The WBP removes the advantage of you receiving a benefit representing a higher percentage of your earnings, plus a pension from a job at which you did not pay Social Security taxes.

HOW BIG WILL MY SOCIAL SECURITY BENEFIT BE?

The size of your full Social Security benefit will vary depending on (among other things) what year you were born and what year you begin claiming your benefit. For example, if you were born between 1943 and 1954, you can receive only 75 percent of your full benefit at age 62, or 100 percent of your full benefit at age 66. If you were born 1960 or later, you can receive 70 percent of your full benefit at age 62, or 100 percent of your full benefit at age 67. You can receive your *maximum* benefit by waiting until age 70 to take it.

If you're an older American worker, you should be receiving an annual statement from the Social Security Administration that estimates your Social Security retirement benefit at age 62, at your full retirement age, and at age 70. You should check these statements for accuracy, including all your personal information and your earnings history. If you have not received your statement, you can submit a request by calling 1-800-772-1213 or visiting www.ssa.gov.

But your estimated benefit may not tell the whole story. If you start drawing your benefit prior to reaching your full retirement age, and continue earning income, your benefits may be reduced. Until you reach your full retirement age, your benefit will be reduced by $1 for every $2 you *earn* over a set limit (which rises annually) in annual income and $1 for every $3 earned over a higher set limit. *Earned* income does not include income you receive from your pension, investments, or rental property—as long as you are not a real estate professional. One thing to keep in mind is that this benefit reduction is not permanent. The first year in which your earnings do not exceed the set limit, your benefit will resume to the level it was before the reduction. The earnings limit goes away once you reach full retirement age; at this you can earn as much as Bill Gates and continue receiving your full benefit.

To see how reductions in your Social Security benefit can impact your retirement income, consider John–who retired at age 62 and who is now 63. He has a benefit of $18,000 per year, but decides to return to work on a part-time basis. The earnings limitation in 2018 is $17,040 (go to ssa.gov to see current year's limitation). The first year he earns $10,000, so his benefit is not affected at all and his total income that year is $28,000. In the second year he earns $20,000, which is $2,960, so his Social Security benefit is reduced $1 for each dollar over the earnings limit ($17,040). John's benefit will be reduced for that year only by $1,480, 50% of $2,960. If your earned income exceeds $45,360, then your benefit is reduced by $1 for every $3 above the income limit. One simple way to avoid these benefit reductions is to wait until you reach your full retirement age to begin taking your benefits. It's important to emphasize two things-full retirement age (at which time the earnings limits go away) and what is "earned income". Earned income is truly earnings from a job, not earnings from investments or other passive income, like rental properties or royalty income.

One thing to keep in mind is that if you begin drawing a reduced Social Security check before your full retirement age, and earn more money than the annual income limit—thus reducing your Social Security benefit—that smaller benefit does not represent lost dollars per se. That's because Social Security will give you a *delayed credit* for the amount that your benefit was decreased, meaning that amount will continue to increase by 8 percent a year until you stop earning more than set limit. When you do reach that point, your benefit will actually be higher than it was when you started working part-time in the first place.

HOW SOCIAL SECURITY BENEFITS ARE TAXED

Surprisingly, many people don't realize that if your earned income is high enough, your Social Security retirement benefit is taxed. If you are a single person, head of household, or qualifying widower who's Modified Adjusted Gross Income or MAGI (essentially one half of your Social Security plus all your other reportable income, including tax-free interest on bonds) is between $25,000 and $34,000, then up to 50 percent of your Social Security benefit check can be taxed. If your MAGI is more than $34,000 up to 85 percent of your benefit can be taxed. If you're a married couple filing jointly the limit is $32,000 to $44,000, before up to 50 percent of your benefit is subject to taxation, and more than $44,000 before as 85 percent of your benefit can be taxed.

When we talk about the percent of your benefit that can be taxed we are *not* talking about the percent of tax you actually have to pay. Because the taxation of Social Security benefits is calculated differently than taxable income, we advise you to consult a tax professional or certified public account for details. Here's one more thing to keep in mind. Though not required, you may choose to have federal income taxes withheld from your monthly benefit check to avoid paying quarterly estimated tax payments.

THE FUTURE OF SOCIAL SECURITY

Unless you've been marooned on a desert island for the past decade, you know some changes must be made to the Social Security program to maintain its solvency. The non-partisan Congressional Budget Office says that unless significant adjustments are made, the Social Security trust fund will be exhausted by 2033. Five years ago, the CBO projected that would occur in 2042, so Social Security's so-called Day of Reckoning may be closer than 2033.

Why the dire predictions? In a word, demographics. In 1945, the ratio of workers to Social Security beneficiaries was 41.9 to 1. In 2011, there were only 2.9 workers supporting each person receiving Social Security benefits. Right now 10,000 boomers a day are turning 65, and by 2035, the projected ratio of workers to Social Security beneficiaries will be 2.0 to 1.[16]

Why is this important? Because Social Security is a pay-as-you-go system. The Social Security check you're now receiving is not being paid with money you've put into the system via the payroll tax, but with tax money current workers are putting into the system. So if there is a dramatic dip in the number of workers, as is prognosticated by most pundits, then paying those Social Security checks in full will become problematic.

No age group is more aware of Social Security's ills than young people. A recent poll found that more Americans under age 45 believe aliens exist than believe Social Security will be there when they become eligible. [17]Things may not be that bleak, but consider this: For the next two decades, the combined cost rate for the *Old-Age and Survivors Insurance Trust Fund* and the *Disability Insurance Trust Fund* is projected to rise rapidly due to these demographic trends. The OASI is used to pay monthly benefits to retired-worker beneficiaries and their spouses and children; and to survivors of deceased insured workers. The Disability Insurance Trust Fund is used to pay monthly benefits to disabled-

---

[16] 2012 Social Security Administration report.
[17] USA Today poll.

worker beneficiaries and their spouses and children; and to provide rehabilitation services to the disabled. By 2033, the two funds are projected to be exhausted, meaning that beneficiaries would receive about 75 percent of their scheduled benefits.[18]

The cost rate of these two funds will increase even more sharply over the next five years, thanks to a recession that is reducing the tax base through high unemployment and causing the number of Social Security beneficiaries to surge. Any time the economy tanks, there is a predictable spike in the number of people applying for Social Security retirement benefits earlier than they'd planned (often due to the unexpected loss of a job), as well as an increase in the number of people applying for Social Security disability benefits. When my (David's) Dad turned 65 and went to the Social Security office to sign up for Medicare, he told me that "there were more young people in there trying to get on disability than there were old farts like me."

Thankfully, the federal government recognizes that changes are necessary to keep the program financially afloat. In fact, Social Security has already made a few changes—such as raising the full retirement ages of those born in 1938 or later (it's now as high as 67 for those born in 1960 or after), and lowering the percentage of the full retirement benefit you receive if you begin taking them at age 62. Going forward, government officials are now talking about possibly raising the full retirement age even higher, reducing cost-of-living increases, modifying the benefit formula to reduce basic benefits, and increasing the 6.2 percent payroll tax.

---

[18] Congressional Budget Office.

Today's Guide to Retirement Planning

There's another possible change that we haven't heard as much about, but we feel it's a strong possibility. It's called *means testing*, a process by which the government determines that if you have the means (if you have a certain level of income or assets or both), then your scheduled Social Security benefit will be reduced, or a larger portion of it will be taxed. But regardless of what changes are made to Social Security, whether it's means testing or the reduction of cost-of-living increases or whatever, they will probably not impact those 55 and older.

And as we look into our crystal ball at Social Security's long-term future, we see a ray of hope hovering on the horizon—thanks to the children of the boomers. Called *echo boomers* because they are the demographic echo of their parents, they represent the largest generation of young people since the '60s. Born between 1982 and 1995, they number nearly 80 million, almost a third of the U.S. population.[19] The youngest are still in grade school and the oldest are just out of college, and when this tsunami of humanity enters the work force and begins paying payroll taxes, it will have the same effect on Social Security that a performance-enhancing drug has on an Olympic athlete.

Employer-sponsored retirement plans

Another source of retirement income for many of us comes from employer-sponsored retirement plans, the most common of which are *qualified retirement plans*—plans that are given favorable tax treatment by the IRS and apply equally to all employees in a company. These plans, provided to workers as an employee benefit, are offered by 78

---

[19] U.S. Census Bureau.

percent of U.S. private companies with more than 100 employees and 43 percent of private companies with fewer than 100 employees.[20]

If your company offers such a plan, you should definitely participate. It's a powerful savings tool for retirement. While every plan is unique, they all fall into one of two general categories—*defined benefit plans* and *defined contribution plans.*

DEFINED BENEFIT PLANS

A defined benefit plan, commonly referred to as a pension, does what the name implies. It provides you with a defined benefit—usually in the form of a monthly payout. Typically, you don't put your own money into this plan or make investment choices. Rather, your public or private employer pumps money into it on your behalf and decides how to invest it. In return, your employer pledges to give you a defined monthly retirement benefit at a specified time in the future— often calculating your benefit by using a formula that factors in your salary and years of service. Normally, most or all of your earned benefit is guaranteed by federal insurance provided by through the Pension Benefit Guaranty Corporation (PBGC).

Many employees like defined benefit plans because of that guarantee, but also because they don't have to put any money into the plans, they know in advance what their retirement benefit will be, and they don't have to worry about making investment decisions because the plan's assets are managed by professional money managers. What's more, the money in the plan grows tax-deferred, and the employer may even offer cost-of-living adjustments to the defined benefit.

---

[20] U.S. Bureau of Labor Statistics.

But not everyone is smitten by defined benefit plans, commonly called pensions. Some find the plans difficult to fully understand, or aren't comfortable with the fact that the plans rarely benefit employees who leave the company before they retire, typically don't offer a lump sum payment at retirement, and may provide only a portion of the funds they need for retirement. Some defined benefit plans don't begin paying any benefits until the employee reaches normal retirement age, while others offer a reduced benefit if you quit before the normal retirement age.

Defined benefit plans are rapidly going the way of the dodo bird, so if you are among the fortunate few who can participate in such a plan, you should take advantage of it. The number of private employers offering traditional defined benefit plans has been plummeting for years. A decade ago, 32 percent of private industry companies offered defined benefit plans. By 2012, only 17 percent offered such plans.[21]

The reason for the decline is that defined benefit plans obligate companies to pay a specified benefit to employees for the rest of their lives. Because the lifespan of Americans is on the rise, this can lead to a staggering sum of unfunded pension obligations. This financial albatross is one of the factors that bankrupted General Motors.

DEFINED CONTRIBUTION PLANS

A defined contribution plan, such as 401(k) or 403(b), defines the amount of money an employee contributes to the plan (usually a percentage of your gross salary), as well as any matching contribution the company might make on the employee's behalf. In private industry, defined contribution plans have become increasingly in vogue in recent years as defined benefit plans have fallen out of favor. A decade ago,

---

[21] U.S. Bureau of Labor Statistics.

only 35 percent of private companies offered defined contribution plans. By 2012, that figure had risen to 41 percent.[22] This trend places more responsibility on employees to decide how much money they contribute to the plan, as well as how they want the money to be invested. We recommend contributing at least enough money to qualify for the full match offered by the company, if the company does indeed offer a match.

With a defined contribution plan, your benefits are based solely on the amount of money you contribute to the plan—plus or minus any gains or losses to the account due to the performance of your investments. The plan also provides you with your own individual account that's separate from the accounts of your coworkers, unlike a defined benefit plan in which all the money is pooled together. You must take minimum annual distributions after age 70½, just as you must with an IRA or defined benefit plan, and any money you withdraw from the account during retirement its usually taxed as ordinary income.

Many employees like defined contribution plans because they are easy to understand, provide tax-deferred growth, and allow them to decide how much they want to contribute—up to a specified maximum percentage or amount. They also like the possibility of making big gains through astute investment choices, and the freedom to make their contributions through payroll deductions—which they find less painful because they never see the money. Another advantage is that there are a variety of ways they can withdraw the money when it comes time to do so.

But defined contribution plans are not without drawbacks. For one thing, the amount of your annual contributions are limited either by

---

[22] U.S. Bureau of Labor Statistics.

law or the plan. For another, these plans don't assure you a specific retirement benefit because that benefit will be largely determined by the performance of your investments. And when it comes to projecting what that benefit will be, we feel compelled to offer a word of caution. Not long ago I (David) was talking to a firefighter who had $70,000 in his defined contribution retirement account. He said he kept calling up the plan representative, who repeatedly told him that if his contributions and investment performance continued on their current course, he would have $600,000 in his account when he reached his full retirement age in 10 years. He said that sounded wonderful, but he was skeptical. I crunched the numbers for him, and found that even if his investments grew 8 percent a year for the next decade, his account would grow to only $290,000.

TYPES OF DEFINED CONTRIBUTION PLANS

There are many types of defined contribution plans. Though they all have a lot in common, each has some unique characteristics that separate it from the rest. It's up to you to make sure you know what type of defined contribution plan you have. The other day a client came into the office saying he wanted to borrow money from his 401(k) plan to buy a piece of property alongside his house. We spent hours talking about how to accomplish this in the most effective way before we discovered that he didn't have a 401(k) plan at all, but a "Saving Incentive Match Plans for Employees" or SIMPLE plan (which we'll explain a little later in this chapter). What did that mean? It meant that all our calculations were a waste of time, because you can't take a loan from a SIMPLE plan. Here's a quick look at some of the more common defined contribution plans:

401 (K) PLANS

The 401(k) plan, the most prevalent of all the defined contribution plans, allows you to contribute pre-tax dollars into the plan, thus reducing your taxable income. You typically contribute to the plan through payroll deductions, and those contributions and earnings will grow tax-deferred until you withdraw them. Normally, you're allowed to change your investment selections (which are managed by financial professionals), as well as your beneficiary (as long as your spouse concurs). Fees are built into the plan, and some employers will match a percentage of your contributions.

Your contributions to a 401(k) plan are limited, either by law or the plan itself. The law prohibits you from contributing more per year than your annual salary; and there is an annual contribution limit. Those 50 years or older can make additional "catch-up" contributions up to a set amount per year. The total combination of employee contributions, employer contributions, and profit-sharing amounts are limited to the lesser of 100 percent of an employee's annual compensation and a set figure, which the government changes from time to time. You must begin taking annual required minimum distributions from your account after age 70½.

Some 401(k) plans allow you to make contributions to a Roth-401(k) account. Those contributions will be taxed up front, but qualified distributions from that account will be tax-free. You can also convert the money in your 401(k) plan to a Roth 401(k) plan at any time (provided a Roth plan is available), but you must pay income taxes in the year of the conversion.

Some 401(k) plans automatically enroll employees in the plan, unless they elect otherwise, by reducing their pay to fund their contributions. But these plans must provide a notice to participants that explain their right to opt out of the plan or change the rate of contribution, and detail the time periods for making elections and how their contributions will be invested in the absence of the participants' direction. Some of these "automatic" plans give employees a 90-day window to elect out of the plan and withdraw automatic contributions and related earnings without having to pay a 10 percent early withdrawal penalty.

One nice thing about 401(k) plans is that 100 percent of your contributions and investment earnings are *vested*, meaning you get to keep them even if you are terminated or choose to leave your company. (The vested percentage refers to the portion of your account that cannot be reclaimed by your employer). Your employer's contributions to your 401(k) may become vested over time on either a graded or cliff-vesting schedule.

Though withdrawals you make upon retirement from your 401(k) account are taxed as ordinary income, non-qualified withdrawals made prior to age 59½ are subject to a 10 percent tax penalty plus income tax. You can make penalty-free withdrawals if you become disabled, leave your employer in the calendar year you turn 55 or after, or retire before age 55 and take *Substantially Equal Periodic Payments*—a series of substantially equal periodic payments that must continue for five years or until you reach age 59½, whichever is later. You are also allowed to take loans against your 401(k) account, subject to restrictions; and your beneficiary can make penalty-free withdrawals from the account upon your death.

403 (B) PLANS

If you work for a public school or a tax-exempt organization, you can participate in a 403(b) plan, which used to be called a *tax-sheltered annuity*. You can contribute pre-tax dollars, usually through a payroll deduction, and those contributions and earnings will grow tax-deferred until you withdraw them. Your professionally-managed investment choices will include fixed and variable annuities through insurance companies, and sometimes a custodial account made up of 403(b)(7) mutual funds. Some employers will match your contributions to the plan, and you can take loans against your account, subject to restrictions.

Fees are built into the plan, and you can change your beneficiary at any time— though your spouse's permission is required if you have a plan that's subject to the *Employee Retirement Income Security Act of 1974*, a federal law that sets minimum standards for pension plans in private industry.

By law, your contributions cannot exceed 100 percent of your annual compensation. You contribute up to a set amount set by the government, but if you are 50 years of age or older you can make additional "catch-up" contributions to the plan. If you have 15 or more years of experience for the same employer, even if those years are not consecutive, you can contribute an additional amount per year, as long as the average of your previous contributions did not exceed a set figure. The combined amount of employee and employer contributions is limited to the lesser of a set amount and 100 percent of an employee's annual compensation.

Some 403(b) plans allow you to make contributions to a Roth 403(b) account. These contributions will be taxed, but qualified distributions from your account will be tax-free. Amounts in your 403(b) plan can be converted to Roth 403(b) plans (if available) at any time, but income taxes must be paid in the year of the conversion.

With a 403(b) plan, 100 percent of your contributions and investment earnings are *vested*. And any of your contributions to the plan may become vested over time on either a graded or cliff-vesting schedule.

You must begin taking annual required minimum distributions after age 70½. Non-qualified withdrawals prior to age 59½ are subject to a 10 percent tax penalty in addition to income tax, and withdrawals at retirement are taxed as ordinary income. Penalty-free withdrawals can be made if you become disabled or leave your employer in the calendar year you turn 55 or after; or retire before age 55 and take distributions as "Substantially Equal Periodic Payments" for five years or until you reach 59½, whichever is later. Your beneficiary can make penalty-free withdrawals from the account upon your death.

SEP-IRA

This IRA allows employers, including those who are self-employed, to make tax-favored contributions to IRAs owned by employees. The plan must include all employees who are at least age 21, been employed by the employer for at least 3 out of the last 5 years, and meet compensation requirements.

Contributions and earnings are tax-deferred until withdrawn, and the employer's voluntary contributions can be changed or discontinued each year. Annual contributions by an employer on behalf of an employee cannot exceed the lesser of a set amount and 25 percent of the employee's compensation (not to exceed a much larger amount). Though employers are not allowed to set up salary-reduction SEP plans, employers who already had a "Salary Reduction Simplified Employee Pension Plan (SARSEP)—a SEP plan that permits employee salary reduction contributions—may continue to allow salary-reduction contributions by employees.

Employee contribution deductibility and distributions from the plan follow traditional IRA guidelines, and all employer and employee contributions, as well as earnings, are 100 percent vested. You must begin taking annual required minimum distributions before April 1 of the year after you turn 70 ½.

SIMPLE PLANS

Savings Incentive Match Plans for Employees (SIMPLE), which takes the form of an IRA or a 401(k), is a retirement plan set up by some employers with 100 or fewer employees. Employers can start a SIMPLE plan only if they contribute to the plan and they do not maintain another qualified plan. All employees who earn above a set amount per year can participate, and they can make pre-tax contributions. The contributions and earnings are tax-deferred until withdrawn. The law mandates that employee contributions do not exceed 100 percent of the employee's annual compensation. Workers can contribute a set amount per year, and those 50 or older can make an additional "catch-up" contribution up to a set limit. You can take loans against your account, subject to restrictions.

Employers are generally required to contribute to the plan in one of two ways— by matching an employee's elective contributions dollar-for-dollar up to a limit of 3 percent of the employee's compensation, or by making a non-elective contribution of 2 percent of each eligible employee's compensation, whether or not the employee chooses to make any contributions. Employee and employer contributions, as well as earnings, are 100 percent vested.

Any withdrawals you make in retirement are taxed as ordinary income. Distributions within the first two years of participation are subject to a 25 percent penalty tax; and distributions after the first two years of participation, but before age 59½, are subject to a 10 percent penalty tax. You must begin taking annual required minimum distributions before April 1 of the year after your turn 70½.

457 PLANS

A 457 plan is a deferred-compensation plan specifically designed for state and local governments; and for private, tax-exempt organizations. It generally offers several types of investments to choose from, and it does not have to apply equally to all employees. Employees can contribute pre-tax dollars to their account, and the contributions and earnings are tax-deferred until withdrawn.

The amount of an employee's contributions is limited either by the law or the plan. The law says an employee's annual contribution can't exceed the employee's annual compensation. Participants can contribute no more than a set amount a year to the account, but those 50 years or older can make up to a certain dollar amount a year in additional "catch-up" contributions.

Few 457 plans offer a match, because matching or employer contributions reduce the salary deferral limit in the year in which they are vested. But they do offer a "final three year" provision if you are within the three years prior to your "normal" retirement age (as defined by the plan) and have not contributed the maximum amount in prior years. The provision allows you to contribute your normal limit for the year plus unused amounts from prior years, up to a maximum dollar figure or 200 percent of the elective deferral limit.

If you have enough includable compensation, you can contribute the maximum elective deferral limit to a 457(b), 401(k) or 403(b) plan. If you're 50 years or older, you can also make "catch-up" contributions.

Your contributions and earnings are 100 percent vested. Federal law doesn't impose any requirements on the vesting of employer contributions in governmental 457 plans, but vesting is subject to any state law mandates or restrictions. In the absence of any state restrictions, the employer can establish a vesting schedule to govern employer contributions. Your contributions are not subject to federal income taxes, but they may be subject to FICA in the year they become vested. You can't access your vested funds to pay for this tax liability, but many state and local government employees are not subject to FICA.

You must begin taking annual required minimum distributions before April 1 of the year after you turn 70½. Before age 59½, any payouts you receive are generally *not* subject to a 10 percent tax penalty, but you'll pay a 10 percent tax penalty on any withdrawal you make that is "attributable to" a rollover from a qualified plan 403(b) plan. You are not allowed to take any plan distributions prior to your termination of employment, even if you're over 59½. Some 457 plans permit you to make a pre-retirement withdrawal to pay for an "unforeseeable emergency." The plan sponsor deals with these early withdrawal requests on a case-by-case basis, taking into account such things as the nature of the emergency and other financial resources available to you.

Choosing your beneficiary

Whether you participate in an IRA, Roth IRA, or employer-sponsored retirement plan, it's crucial that you fill out the beneficiary form on your retirement account. It's the document that directs where your money goes when you die. It has kingly clout, overriding all other documents, including your will. That's why you should choose your beneficiary, or beneficiaries, wisely—and let your loved ones know where your beneficiary document is stored. Should things change in your life, such as a divorce or the death of your beneficiary, be sure to revise your beneficiary document to reflect those changes.

IF YOU HAVE A DEFINED CONTRIBUTION PLAN AND SELECT AS YOUR BENEFICIARY:

- Your spouse, then your surviving spouse beneficiary can transfer death distributions to a traditional IRA and treat it as his or her own IRA. In some cases, your surviving spouse may be able to leave money in the plan and take distributions as allowed by the plan. If you're the surviving spouse, you have the option of taking the death distribution as a beneficiary or as a spouse. Let's say you're 50 years old and your husband dies. If you take his retirement account as a surviving spouse, then you'd face the same restrictions for withdrawing the money that any 50-year-old would face when pulling money from a retirement account. But if you take the distribution as a beneficiary, there would be no restrictions on your withdrawals.

- A non-spouse, then your non-spouse beneficiary can have death distributions transferred directly to "inherited IRAs," or convert those distributions to "inherited Roth IRAs." Non-spouse

beneficiaries could be your children, grandchildren, siblings, nieces, nephews, cousins, even friends.
- No one, then the plan's money is paid to your estate—where it is subject to probate, the terms of your will, and possibly the claims of your creditors. Let's say you die with $200,000 in your retirement account, and you'd named some beneficiaries in your will but had not listed any beneficiaries on your beneficiary form. Then the money is dumped into your estate, and the income tax on that money—let's say $80,000—is immediately due, leaving $120,000 in the account to be distributed among the beneficiaries named in your will. But if you had named your beneficiaries directly on the form, they would be able to defer the taxes on the $200,000 instead of paying them right away.

IF YOU HAVE A TRADITIONAL IRA AND SELECT AS YOUR BENEFICIARY:

- Your spouse, then your spouse can transfer the death distributions to his or her own IRA, or transfer the account's assets to an "inherited IRA."
- A non-spouse, then the non-spouse can transfer the assets to an "inherited IRA."
- No one, then the money is payable to your estate and is subject to probate, the terms of your will, and possibly the claims of your creditors.

IF YOU HAVE A DEFINED BENEFIT PLAN:

- Check your plan document carefully to determine what benefits are available to your beneficiaries. Defined benefit plans are required to provide a "Qualified Pre-Retirement Survivor

Annuity" or a "Qualified Joint and Survivor Annuity" that provides lifetime pension payments to the beneficiary. When you retire you will have to select one of various options that will determine what percent of your monthly retirement benefit will go to your beneficiary (usually your spouse) should you die. The higher percentage you want your beneficiary to have, the lower your monthly benefit. Keep in mind that this is an irrevocable decision. Once you make it, it's final.

> "We as Americans focus too much on net worth, but forget about net income."
> -Doug Hughes

5
RETIREMENT PLAN DISTRIBUTIONS

"For most of my life I've concentrated on putting money *into* my retirement nest egg, but now that I'm retired I don't know the best way to take it *out*."

That is one of the most common statements we hear from our clients. And it's certainly understandable. Making smart investments can be complex and nuanced, but making shrewd withdrawals from your retirement plans can be even more so. In this chapter we will look at ways you can minimize taxes and avoid penalties when you withdraw money from your retirement plan, explain how you can gain early access to your retirement funds, and outline the rules regarding required minimum distributions.

Required minimum distributions

Required minimum distributions (RMDs) are minimum amounts you must withdraw annually from your retirement plan account. Generally, you must begin making withdrawals before April 1 of the year after you turn 70½. If you are still working for your employer, and don't own at least 5 percent of the business sponsoring the plan, you don't have to start taking distributions from that employer's plan until April 1 of the year after you retire. If you don't take your required minimum distributions on time, you'll have to pay a tax penalty of 50 percent of the difference between the required and actual distribution. The rules regarding required minimum distributions apply to employer-sponsored retirement plans, traditional IRAs, IRA-based plans, and Roth 401(k) accounts, but do *not* apply to Roth IRAs while the owner is still alive.

At age 70 ½ your required minimum distribution would be 3.65 percent of your December 31st account value. Each year after that, the percent would climb—from 4.37 percent at age 75 to 5.35 percent at age 80 to 8.77 percent at age 90. If you make it to 115 or beyond, the percent jumps to 52.63 percent—but at that age, who would really care?

You compute your annual minimum distribution by using a standardized *distribution period* in years, which is *not* your life expectancy. The distribution period is 27.4 years at age 70, and decreases each year after that—to 26.5 years at age 71, 22.9 years at age 75, and 11.4 years at age 90. If you are age 70 and have $100,000 in your retirement account, for example, you would calculate your minimum distribution by dividing $100,000 by 27.4 to get $3,650—which represents 3.65 percent of your $100,000.

One thing to note is that you can transfer some or all of your IRA directly to a qualified charity and it would not be included in your taxable income and would go toward satisfying your RMD. The maximum annual amount you can send directly to charity is $100,000 per year. Recently one of our clients with a $1 million IRA said he wanted to give $50,000 a year for the next five years to his church building fund. So each year we had him transfer $50,000 directly from his IRA to his church. The $50,000 was not included in his taxable income, and it easily satisfied his minimum distributions required by law. This strategy is called a "Qualified Charitable Distribution." [23]

Defined benefit plans

Defined benefit plans, often referred to as *pensions*, are *qualified* retirement plans. Qualified plans receive favorable tax treatment and are regulated by the Employee Retirement Income Security Act. These plans, offered by public or private employers, provide you with tax-deferred savings. They don't require you to make any investment selections, and promise you a specified monthly benefit at retirement if you're an eligible employee. Some employers will define this benefit as an exact dollar amount you will receive at retirement, but most calculate it by using a formula that considers factors such as your salary and years of service.

Benefits from these plans are normally not paid until you reach your normal retirement age – which is 65 years old for most plans–though some plans allow you to take a smaller distribution if you retire before your normal retirement age. Rather than offering you a lump sum distribution at retirement, most defined benefit plans provide you with monthly annuity payments.

Defined contribution plans

Defined contribution plans, such as the 401(k) and 403(b), are also qualified retirement plans that provide you with tax-deferred retirement

---

[23] https://www.irs.gov/retirement-plans/retirement-plans-faqs-regarding-iras-distributions-withdrawals

savings. But they provide you with your own individual account into which you, your employer, or both, can contribute. You will usually be responsible for making your own investment selections, and your benefits are based on the amount of money you contribute to your account—plus or minus expenses, gains or losses.

LEAVE THE MONEY OR MOVE IT?

When you retire or change jobs, you can leave your money in your defined contribution plan (if that is allowed by the plan), where it will retain its tax-deferred status and not incur any penalties. But that would prevent you from making more contributions to the plan and limit your investment choices to those offered by the plan. In addition, your plan may change if your former employer is purchased or merges with another company.

Leaving your money in a defined contribution plan also will saddle you with the responsibility of having to continue monitoring the account; and if you have another retirement benefit plan through your new employer, you will have to take separate, annual required minimum distributions from each plan when you pass the 70½-year-old threshold. What's more, you are not allowed to aggregate your qualified plans and your IRAs in determining how much your required minimum distribution is, and after you die your heirs will encounter delays and paperwork having the money transferred to an IRA.

The IRS gives you another compelling reason to not leave your money parked in your plan by making less flexible rules for defined contribution plans than for IRA accounts. For example, you can take a penalty-free withdrawal from your IRA account in order to pay for qualified education expenses or first-time home buying expenses—whereas those kinds of withdrawals from a defined contribution plan will incur a 10 percent tax penalty.

So if you don't leave the money in your defined contribution plan, what do you do with it? You have basically four choices—transfer the money to your new employer's plan if that's allowed by the plan, transfer the money into a traditional IRA, receive a lump-sum distribution, or receive monthly annuity payments if allowed by the plan.

Many people make a costly mistake when they change jobs by taking the money in cash, and are forced as a result to pay tax penalties and lose potential tax-deferred growth. A survey showed that 46 percent of employees, when switching to a new job, took their defined contribution plan benefits in cash, while 29 percent kept their savings in their current employer's 401(k) plan and 25 percent rolled the money over into a qualified IRA or other retirement plan.[24]

Here are your options:

- New employer's plan—If you transfer money to your new employer's plan you can continue making contributions, avoid penalties, and preserve the money's tax-deferred status. But because the plan will have limited investment choices, it will shackle your flexibility.
- Traditional IRA—If you transfer the money into a traditional IRA, you can continue making IRA contributions and choose from a virtually unlimited number of investment opportunities. You will avoid any penalties and your money will retain its tax-deferred status. You will eventually have to take required

---

[24] 2009 analysis by AON Hewitt.

minimum distributions, and pay income taxes when you withdraw the money.
- Lump-sum distribution—If you choose to receive a lump-sum distribution rather than monthly payments, you will receive the plan's entire account balance. But you will have to pay taxes on the money, and certain penalties might apply if conditions are not met. Some plans allow you to take a lump sum payment and immediately roll it over into an IRA, allowing you to avoid paying taxes on the money until you withdraw it from the IRA.
- Monthly annuity payments—If you choose to receive monthly annuity payments, you must select an annuity income option, such as *single life,* or *joint and survivor.* The annuity is tax-deferred, and the payments are guaranteed for life if the company or insurance company issuing the annuity remains financially healthy, but you will have to pay income tax on the payments you receive. The annuity option does not give you emergency access to your principal or provide you with an inflation hedge, but it does give you the assurance of fixed distributions for life—which many people find attractive.

MAKING AN IRA TRANSFER

Many people make a colossal blunder when transferring money from a defined contribution plan to a traditional IRA by having their former employer give them a check made payable to themselves. If the check is made payable to you and you deposit it into a traditional IRA account, a procedure known as a *rollover,* the federal government will withhold 20 percent of that money to ensure that you actually do put the money into an IRA. And unless you have additional outside funds to pay 20 percent of that rollover amount within 60 days, you will owe income tax on the amount withheld and—If you're under age 59½—you have to pay a 10 percent early withdrawal penalty on it as well.

To avoid all these taxes and penalties, you should insist on a *direct rollover*, a procedure in which your former employer sends you a check made payable to your IRA *custodian* (the vendor you've selected to hold your IRA account), and you send the check to your custodian for deposit into your traditional IRA account; or insist on a *transfer*, in which your former employer sends a check payable to your IRA custodian directly to the custodian for deposit into your traditional IRA account. It doesn't matter whether the check is sent to you or your IRA's custodian, as long as it's made payable to the IRA custodian.

To see how costly it is to make an IRA transfer mistake, consider Bill, who upon retiring at age 54 rolled over the $100,000 in his defined contribution plan by asking for the check to be made payable to himself. The mandatory 20 percent tax withholding took an immediate $20,000 bite out of the account, leaving it with a balance of $80,000. He had to pay 25 percent federal tax ($5,000) on the $20,000, plus a 10 percent early withdrawal penalty ($2,000)—leaving him with a net income tax refund of $13,000.

Robert, on the other hand, retired at the same age as Bill and with the same $100,000 in his defined benefit plan. But Robert executed a transfer in which the $100,000 check was made payable to his IRA custodian and sent to the custodian, who deposited it into Robert's traditional IRA account. Robert paid no taxes or penalties, and after just one year of earning 8 percent interest, his $100,000 account had grown to $108,000.

Here's another good reason to avoid rolling over the money in your retirement plan into an IRA. If you quit or are fired from your job, the year you turn 55 you can take money out of your qualified retirement plan without having to pay the 10 percent early withdrawal penalty because you are under the 59½ year-old threshold. You will still have to pay taxes on the money, but not a penalty. The moment you put that rolled over money into an IRA, however, you are subject to the 59½-year-old early withdrawal penalty.

NET UNREALIZED APPRECIATION

If the company you work for offers a profit sharing, 401(k), or stock bonus plan that includes company securities, you may be eligible for an often-overlooked provision in tax law that can provide you with significant income tax savings. It's called *"net unrealized appreciation,"* and it allows you to pay long-term capital gains tax on part of your account when you change jobs or retire.

Here is how it works. You simply ask for the company securities to be distributed in kind (as shares, not cash) to your taxable brokerage account as part of a total distribution from the plan. You'll pay ordinary income tax on the original cost of the securities, but not on their worth. The difference between the cost basis and the stock's market value when you receive the distribution will be taxed as long-term capital gains in the year that you sell the company securities. Any change in value after you receive the distribution will be taxed as long-or short-term capital gain or loss, depending on how long you hold the securities. But this tax treatment is not available if the company securities are transferred to an IRA or converted to a Roth IRA.

To illustrate how this might work, let's look at Emily, who has a 401(k) balance of $300,000, and $100,000 of that amount is company stock (matching employer contributions) with a cost basis of $10,000. When Emily retires, she tells the 401(k) plan administrator to transfer the shares of company stock to her brokerage account as a taxable transaction, and to transfer the other assets into her traditional IRA account. The $10,000 will be taxed as ordinary income and the tax will be due when she receives her distribution. The $90,000 will be taxed as long-term capital gains and that tax will be due when the stock is sold. And any change in value after she receives the stock will be taxed as a long-or short-term capital gain or loss, and the tax will be due when the stock is sold.

PENSION INCOME

Whether you have a defined benefit plan or a defined contribution plan, you can generally receive your retirement plan distribution as a monthly annuity—and that income will be taxed as ordinary income. Some retirement plan annuity programs offer a cost-of-living adjustment, and some are insured. The insured plans are safer because it's possible for your employer or insurance company to fall on hard times and be unable to make your monthly payments.

Most annuity programs offer you several choices for you and/or your beneficiaries to receive your monthly payments. You should talk to a financial professional before making your choice, because it's an irrevocable decision. Here are five of the more common choices offered:

- *Single life*—Your monthly payments will be paid to you throughout your entire life. This selection provides you with the largest benefit, but when you die your spouse will receive nothing.

- *Joint and 100 percent survivor*—This benefit will be smaller than the single life option, but you will receive it throughout your life, and when you die your spouse will continue to receive the same benefit until he or she passes away.
- *Joint and 50 percent survivor*—This monthly benefit will be less than the Single Life option but greater than the Joint and 100 Percent Survivor option. It will be paid to you as long as you are alive, and when you die your spouse will receive 50 percent of that benefit for the rest of his or her life.
- *Period certain*—This benefit is paid monthly for a specified number of years, after which the benefit ends. The number of years cannot extend beyond your life expectancy.
- *Life with period certain*—This benefit will be paid to you throughout your entire life. If you die within a specified time period—20 years, for example—your spouse will be paid a benefit amount until the time period ends.

IN-SERVICE DISTRIBUTIONS

Generally speaking, if you take distributions from a retirement plan or traditional IRA prior to age 59½, you must pay the 10 percent tax penalty on the amount you withdraw. But you can make penalty-free withdrawals—called *in-service distributions*—before age 59½ if you die or become disabled, you use the money to pay unreimbursed medical expenses in excess of a certain percentage of your adjusted gross income, or you take substantially equal payments according to IRS Code Section 72(t). Because any in-service distribution will reduce the value of the benefits you'll receive when you retire, you should consult with your financial advisor before making an early withdrawal such as this from your retirement plan.

Another way to take penalty-free withdrawals before age 59 ½ is to take the distributions from a qualified retirement plan (but not a traditional IRA) after your employment ends in the calendar year you turn 55 or older. If you are retiring at age 55 or older and need immediate access to only a portion of your retirement funds, you might think about taking a partial, penalty-free distribution from your qualified plan after retirement and transferring the remaining funds from your qualified plan to your traditional IRA. When you reach age 59½, you'll be able to take penalty-free distributions from your IRA account.

Some plans allow you to transfer a portion of the plan's money to an IRA penalty-free, even if you're still working. You might consider making this move, called an *in-service rollover,* if you want more investment choices, you feel your portfolio is bloated with too much employer stock, or you're concerned about the company's future.

If in-service distributions are allowed, salary deferrals may be eligible after the plan's normal retirement age. You may also receive in-service distributions (including elective deferrals) if you lose your job, even if you continue doing the same job for a different employer after an acquisition, merger, or consolidation.

Before the plan's normal retirement age, the following accounts might be eligible:

- Profit-sharing plans
- Stock bonus plans.

- Employee stock ownership plans, subject to restrictions.
- Rollover contributions from a previous employer's plan.

EARLY WITHDRAWALS USING 72(T)

IRS code section 72(t) says you can withdraw IRA funds penalty-free before age 59½ if you determine substantially equal payments using one of three approved formulas—life expectancy formula, annuitization formula, or amortization formula—then continue making scheduled withdrawals using one of the formulas for at least five years or until age 59½ (whichever is later). If you make a mistake on just one of your scheduled withdrawals, you have to pay a penalty tax (plus interest) on not only that withdrawal but on all the withdrawals you previously made. We've seen people make this mistake and it's not a pretty sight. If you choose either the annuitization or amortization formula and later want to reduce your annual withdrawals, you have a one-time opportunity to change to the life expectancy formula.

To better understand how the three formulas differ, let's consider Julie, a 55-year-old woman who was forced into retirement several years ago. To meet her living expenses, she needs to make annual withdrawals from her $750,000 IRA account, which she plans to take at the end of each year. We'll assume a distribution interest rate of 1 percent and a projected earnings rate of 1 percent. Let's also assume the annuitization and amortization formulas are calculated one time only, and the life expectancy formula is calculated each year.

Using the life expectancy formula, Julie would make a first-year withdrawal of $25,338 that gradually increases to $26,315 over six years, leaving her a remaining balance of $636,822. Using the annuitization formula, she would make annual withdrawals of $29,102, leaving her remaining balance at $617,102. And if she chose the amortization formula, her annual withdrawals of $29,398 would leave her with a remaining balance of $615,282.

STRETCH IRA

A stretch IRA allows a beneficiary to take the smallest amount of money from an IRA account—and at the latest time—that's allowed by law. A stretch IRA is not a product but a process, one that can be applied to any IRA. With a stretch IRA, you can make a withdrawal from the account without paying a penalty, and the remaining money in the account can continue to grow tax-deferred. A stretch IRA can reduce immediate income taxes for the beneficiary and create the potential to receive substantially more from an inherited IRA than receiving a lump sum distribution. In essence, a stretch IRA enables your beneficiaries to maintain the same tax status you have, but they can take their required minimum distributions based on their life expectancy rather than yours.

Why even bother with a stretch IRA? Well, let's assume you leave a $1 million traditional IRA to your 34-year-old son. If he needs the money right away, he would have to pay a huge chunk of taxes on that amount—maybe $350,000 or $400,000. More than likely, he would be forced to dip into his own IRA to pay that hefty tax, which—because the withdrawal would be a taxable distribution—would drain his retirement savings even further. You could avoid this unsavory scenario with a stretch IRA, which would allow your son to take his required minimum distributions based on *his* life expectancy, not yours. That means he can leave the $1 million in the account tax-deferred, allowing it to grow over a period of many years before he has to start taking his minimum distributions at 70½.

Though any IRA can become a stretch IRA, you must name your beneficiary, and that beneficiary must have both a birthday and a pulse. If you leave a stretch IRA to an entity without a birthday and pulse—such as a church or a charity—it creates all kinds of problems. Many people like to leave their retirement accounts to their church or favorite charity because those non-profit organizations will not have to pay the taxes that are due on the account. But because those entities don't have a life expectancy, it makes the execution of the stretch extremely challenging. It can be straightened out by an experienced financial professional, but the repair work must be done by October of the year following the person's death. If you want to leave a portion—let's say 10 percent—of your retirement account to a charity, it's better to simply peel that 10 percent off into a separate IRA and make that charity the sole beneficiary of that money, and make your loved ones the beneficiaries of the rest of the account.

So how does the stretch IRA work in real life? Let's assume 65-year-old Fred has a $100,000 stretch IRA in 2013, and also assume a 6 percent average rate of return per year. Fred doesn't begin taking any required minimum distributions until he is 70½, and he does so for three years before dying, allowing his wife, Susie, to take over the IRA and treat it as her own. She dies four years later, leaving the IRA to their daughter, Hannah, who is now 40 years old. Hannah begins taking her minimum distributions based on a 40-year-old's life expectancy, and because those distributions are relatively small at first, she can leave much of the money in the account, where it can grow tax-deferred for many years.

By the time Hannah takes her final minimum distribution at the age of 83, she will have withdrawn $598,105. Susie, her mother, extracted $25,243; and Fred withdrew $15,522. Together, the three of them were able to take $638,870 in distributions from a $100,000 IRA because it was set up as a stretch IRA. I will tell you the "stretch IRA" had been under attack, legislation had been proposed to eliminate it and go to a forced five-year payout. However under the recently passed tax law, there was no mention of its elimination.

DISTRIBUTION STRATEGIES

Due to longer average life spans, the declining number of defined benefit plans, and greater-than-ever exposure to inflation risk, baby boomers need to have solid retirement income plans featuring well-chosen withdrawal strategies. While the correct plan of action may differ on an individual bases, here is a brief look at three common strategies:

DIVIDENDS AND INTEREST ONLY

If you use this strategy, you will live solely off the interest generated from your bonds and the dividends generated from your stocks. This is a viable option for those with flexible income needs, specific legacy goals, and low risk tolerance. The advantages of using this strategy are that your principal does not become depleted, and you preserve a significant inheritance for your heirs. The disadvantages are that it generates a smaller income stream than some other strategies, and it requires that you have a large initial portfolio. For example, if you wanted an income stream of $50,000 a year, you would probably need an initial portfolio of about $1.3 million dollars. [25]

---

[25] https://www.marketwatch.com/story/how-to-generate-the-income-you-need-in-retirement-2018-01-04

TOTAL RETURN WITH SYSTEMATIC WITHDRAWALS

If you select this strategy, you would first invest in an actively managed portfolio designed to generate dividends, interest, and capital gains. Your portfolio would include a money market fund, and be regularly re-balanced to maintain an ideal asset allocation. If the value of your portfolio goes up, you would move a certain amount of money into your money market fund; and if your portfolio's value goes down you would move less money into your money market fund. To cover your monthly income needs, you would simply transfer money from the money market account to your checking account.

Those using this strategy usually have specific income needs, have moderate to aggressive risk tolerance, and don't mind spending down their principal. The main advantage of using this strategy is that your entire portfolio contributes to the generation of income, while the primary disadvantages are that you must select the optimum re-balancing frequency (which is difficult to do without computer automation), and you expose yourself to *sequence of returns risk*.

To understand "sequence of returns risk," let's first take a look at how different sequences of returns would affect a starting portfolio of $100,000 during the *accumulation* phase of your working life (let's say from age 41 to age 65), with an 8 percent average annual rate of return. If your portfolio's annual returns are -12 percent, -21 percent, and -14 percent during the first three years of this accumulation phase, and 25 percent, 18 percent, and 29 percent during the final three years of the accumulation phase, your nest egg at age 65 would be $684,848. If we reverse the sequence–meaning your portfolio's annual returns are 29 percent, 18 percent and 25 percent during the first three years of your accumulation phase; and -14 percent, -21 percent, and -12 percent during the final three years of the accumulation phase–your nest egg at age 65 would be exactly the same–$684,848.

CHART 1: Factors Affecting Portfolio Results Before Retirement

Age	Annual Return (Portfolio A)	Portfolio A (Year-End Value)	Annual Return (Portfolio B)	Portfolio B (Year-End Value)
41	↓ -12%	$87,695	↑ 29%	$129,491
42	↓ -21%	$69,426	↑ 18%	$152,281
43	↓ -14%	$59,707	↑ 25%	$189,590
44	↑ 22%	$72,984	↓ -6%	$178,404
45	↑ 10%	$80,136	↑ 15%	$204,272
46	↑ 4%	$83,595	↑ 8%	$221,183
47	↑ 11%	$92,707	↑ 27%	$281,124
48	↑ 3%	$95,210	↓ -2%	$274,939
49	↓ -3%	$92,155	↑ 15%	$315,355
50	↑ 21%	$111,507	↑ 19%	$375,272
51	↑ 17%	$130,129	↑ 33%	$498,737
52	↑ 5%	$137,026	↑ 11%	$554,097
53	↓ -10%	$123,597	↓ -10%	$499,795
54	↑ 11%	$137,316	↑ 5%	$526,284
55	↑ 33%	$182,493	↑ 17%	$614,174
56	↑ 19%	$217,167	↑ 21%	$743,150
57	↑ 15%	$249,091	↓ -3%	$719,305
58	↓ -2%	$243,611	↑ 3%	$738,726
59	↑ 27%	$309,629	↑ 11%	$819,247
60	↑ 8%	$335,262	↑ 4%	$854,602
61	↑ 15%	$383,875	↑ 10%	$938,354
62	↓ -6%	$361,226	↑ 22%	$1,147,022
63	↑ 25%	$449,727	↓ -14%	$986,439
64	↑ 18%	$528,878	↓ -21%	$780,941
65	↑ 29%	$684,848	↓ -12%	$684,848
	8%	$684,848	8%	$684,848

This chart illustrates the scenario above: (REF CHART 1)

But when we look at the sequence of returns risk during the *distribution* phase of your life, a poor market performance during the first few years of your retirement can drastically deplete your portfolio. Let's say you begin with a portfolio of $684,848 that is going to earn an annual average rate of return of 8 percent over the next 25 years. At the age of 66 you begin withdrawing 5 percent of that portfolio each year, adjusted for 3 percent annual inflation. If your portfolio's annual returns are 29 percent, 18 percent, and 25 percent the first three years; and -14 percent, -21 percent, and -12 percent the final three years, your total nest egg at age 90 would be $2,622,984. But if we reverse the sequence—meaning your portfolio's annual returns are -12 percent, -21 percent and -14 percent the first three years; and 25 percent, 18 percent, and 29 percent the final three years, your portfolio would have shrunk to 0 by the time you reach 82. [26]

---

[26] https://www.marketwatch.com/story/retirement-the-sequence-of-returns-2013-02-08

Today's Guide to Retirement Planning

CHART 2: Factors Affecting Portfolio Results After Retirement

Age	Annual Return (Portfolio A)	Portfolio A (Year-End Value)	Annual Return (Portfolio B)	Portfolio B (Year-End Value)
66	↓ -12%	$566,337	↑ 29%	$852,571
67	↓ -21%	$413,086	↑ 18%	$967,355
68	↓ -14%	$318,927	↑ 25%	$1,168,029
69	↑ 22%	$352,432	↓ -6%	$1,061,698
70	↑ 10%	$348,431	↑ 15%	$1,177,105
71	↑ 4%	$323,772	↑ 8%	$1,234,855
72	↑ 11%	$318,176	↑ 27%	$1,528,614
73	↑ 3%	$284,653	↓ -2%	$1,452,871
74	↓ -3%	$232,143	↑ 15%	$1,623,066
75	↑ 21%	$236,215	↑ 19%	$1,886,771
76	↑ 17%	$229,644	↑ 33%	$2,461,500
77	↑ 5%	$194,417	↑ 11%	$2,687,327
78	↓ -10%	$126,543	↓ -10%	$2,375,148
79	↑ 11%	$90,304	↑ 5%	$2,450,746
80	↑ 33%	$68,219	↑ 17%	$2,808,226
81	↑ 19%	$27,383	↑ 21%	$3,344,606
82	↑ 15%	$0	↓ -3%	$3,182,338
83	↓ -2%	$0	↑ 3%	$3,211,664
84	↑ 27%	$0	↑ 11%	$3,503,440
85	↑ 8%	$0	↑ 4%	$3,594,592
86	↑ 15%	$0	↑ 10%	$3,885,017
87	↓ -6%	$0	↑ 22%	$4,685,257
88	↑ 25%	$0	↓ -14%	$3,963,710
89	↑ 18%	$0	↓ -21%	$3,070,398
90	↑ 29%	$0	↓ -12%	$2,622,984
	8%	$0	8%	$2,622,984

This chart illustrates the scenario above: REF CHART 2

Bucket system

Though "sequence of returns risk" cannot be eliminated, it can be significantly reduced by using what we call the *bucket system*.

If you employ this system, you would divide your assets into different buckets designed to meet your specific financial needs. Each bucket would have a unique objective, investment approach and distribution strategy. Typically, you would divide your assets into three buckets. A bucket for the income you need now (this year), a bucket for income you will need soon (years 2-to-12) and a bucket for income you'll need later (12-plus years). Your "now" bucket, which would include a money market account, would be managed to maintain at least one year of supplemental income. Your "soon" bucket would be invested in a more fixed or contractual investment to meet your monthly income needs in years 2-to-12. Your "later" bucket is your growth bucket and would be invested in longer-term investments that may fluctuate more frequently.

You might want to opt for the bucket system if you have specific income needs, have moderate risk tolerance, and are not averse to spending down a portion of your principal, while waiting for growth in your later buckets. In addition to reducing sequence of returns risk, those using the bucket system typically find comfort from having their income stream cushioned from the volatility of the market. It's important to have a cash reserve in case you need extra money that isn't part of your income plan. [2]

In Chapter 6 you will read about different types of investments you can use to fill up your buckets.

6

INVESTMENTS

When it comes to your retirement investments, you can forget about finding a sure thing. Oh sure, you can stuff your money inside your bed mattress and go to sleep at night knowing you won't lose your money in a stock market plunge, but inflation would insidiously eat away the buying power of that stashed-away cash. So unless you want to see the value of your hard-earned money shrink like a cotton T-shirt in a high-speed dryer, forget about zero-risk investing. Even billionaire investor Warren Buffet said, "We do not have, never have had, and never will have an opinion about where the stock market will be a year from now." And as I (David) have always put risk into perspective – "you never know how much risk you can take until you've taken too much"…then it's too late!

Some people have a higher risk tolerance than others, so it's helpful to understand how much risk you can handle psychologically. When we were teaching a retirement planning class in the winter of 2009, the stock market was plummeting 300 to 400 points a day en route to an all-time low. Some of our class members looked as if they were ready to find a ledge to leap from, while others seemed more relaxed— convinced the market would eventually rebound. I (Doug) remember one unfazed gentleman who winsomely wrote on our class evaluation form, "I want to go have some beers with Doug Hughes." Now that laid-back guy had a high tolerance for risk.

Investment considerations

Before formulating your investment strategy you must first determine your investment objectives. Do you want your investment principal to grow, provide you with current income, or both? If you put all your money into a growth fund, but you need a stream of income from that fund, you may quickly find yourself in financial distress, if the market goes down while you are withdrawing money —like a dairy farmer who owns a herd of beef cattle. Conversely, if you want to see your investment experience aggressive growth, you don't want to put all your money into an income fund.

You also have to consider your *time horizon*, the amount of time your money will be invested before you need it. If you have a fairly long time horizon, you may be able to take more risk and potentially achieve a greater rate of return. This is because you'll have time to ride out dips in the stock market. But as you get older, that time horizon might shorten, might create a need for you to become more conservative with your investments. You may be tempted to shift your money into a certain type of investment that's currently "hot" and on the rise, but all it takes is some Geo-Political event, a "Yes" or a "No' from the Federal Reserve Chairperson, and the market can drop faster than a stone in a pail of water.

You don't want to become *too* conservative with your investments, of course, because you may be around for 25 or 30 years after retirement and don't want to outlive your money. Your investment advisor can help you construct a coordinated portfolio that provides you with just the right balance of risk and reward—based on your individual needs and goals. This involves taking a look at the investments you currently have—things like retirement plans, mutual funds, stocks, bonds, real estate, business assets, and cash-value insurance. And it has to be more than a cursory look. For example, you may *think* you're diversified because you own a variety of mutual funds within a particular fund family, but if each of those funds' top holdings are the same four or five stocks, you're really not diversified at all. If those stocks take a dive, so will your portfolio.

Using a professional

In the 1990s do-it-yourself investing became all the rage. Day-trading manuals were selling briskly. Folks were exchanging stock tips in grocery stores and at their kids' soccer games. People could get on the Internet and start buying and selling stocks and mutual funds with online brokerages. Back then it seemed like you could do no wrong…

But the dot.com bubble burst of 1999, when many dot.com companies failed completely and the stock market plummeted, underscored the potential pitfalls of self-investing. Today many people realize that it helps to have knowledge and experience to achieve success as an investor. So they allow their investment strategies to be handled by a professional financial advisor, someone who has access to the latest investment research and often has years of investment experience. A professional can protect you from what's called *emotional investing*, the practice of panicking and making impulsive investment decisions when the stock market is struggling rather than staying the course. Knowing you have a trusted and competent financial professional in your corner not only gives you the assurance that your hard-earned savings and investments are in good hands, but frees you up to focus on your families and careers.

Today there are countless investment options—ranging from bonds and mutual funds to variable annuities and exchange-traded funds. A professional can help you select the kinds of investments that meet your retirement goals, help you build a diversified portfolio, and encourage you adhere to a disciplined approach devoid of emotional investing. Many of today's financial advisors use what is called "modern portfolio theory," developed in 1952 by two people who were awarded Nobel Prizes in economic science. Financial professionals use the theory in concert with sophisticated software to construct portfolios for their clients that offer the maximum expected return for a given level of risk.

Cash reserve fund

Before investing, you should put a chunk of money—equal to 6 – 12 months of your living expenses— into an *emergency* or *cash reserve* fund. This is a recommendation by FINRA and many other investor protection groups. This fund, which often takes the form of a bank savings account, certificate of deposit, or money market, and is intended to be a buffer between you and unexpected emergencies— everything from the untimely demise of your furnace or a rotted out roof to a major medical bill. Without an emergency fund, you may have to borrow money or pay a penalty for withdrawing money early from a retirement account. And when you have to sell an investment to pay for a new roof, your roof is managing your money, not you.

Savings accounts offer you unrestricted access to your money and require a low minimum balance, and will generally pay you a small amount of interest. Certificates of deposit, often referred to as CDs, require you to keep your hands off your investment for a specified period of time—usually 30 days to 10 years. They pay a fixed interest rate, which tends to be higher the longer the period of investment. If you withdraw money from your CD before its maturity date you will incur some penalties.

Money market accounts normally require a minimum balance, and offer a variable interest rate and limited check-writing privileges. Money market mutual funds, which also may require a minimum balance, offer variable income by investing in short-term government and corporate debt. Like regular money markets, they offer check-writing privileges.

Savings accounts, CDs, and money market accounts are usually insured by the Federal Deposit Insurance Corporation, which covers $250,000 of all your qualifying accounts in each insured bank, according to FDIC.gov. Higher coverage limits may apply to joint accounts and certain types of trusts, including payable-on-death accounts (subject to restrictions). It's important to note that money market mutual funds are generally not insured by the FDIC or any other government agency. Though these funds seek to preserve the value of your investment at $1 per share, it is possible to lose money by investing in them.

Investment choices

Once you create a cushion of protection with your emergency fund, it's time to invest. But these days there are enough investment opportunities to make your head spin, as if on a swivel. When helping clients develop an investment strategy, we explain there are really only two basic ways to invest—*you are either a "Loaner" or an "Owner".*

When you are an Owner, you own something, like stocks, real estate or gold—often called a *securities* or *equity investments*—you are actually purchasing an ownership stake in an asset or a company with the hope that the asset or company will increase in value, provide you with income, or both. In return for being an owner, you are not given any guaranteed interest on your investment principal, but you do receive the potential to increase the value and growth of your investment plus the possibility of getting distributed profits or dividends. Your returns have the potential to outpace inflation, but you can lose money if your company performs poorly or your asset drops in value. If you'd put $10,000 in a popular technology company 35 years ago, you might be a millionaire today. But if you'd put that same $10,000 in a non-existent company or one that went bankrupt (remember the auto industry?), you'd have virtually none of that money left.

A less risky investment approach is to loan your money—usually to a bank, a company, or the government. When you put money into a savings account or certificate of deposit, you are in effect loaning the bank your money. The same holds true for bonds. Though some talk about *purchasing* bonds, you are actually becoming a creditor when you acquire bonds. In return for your loan, the borrower promises to repay your principal investment and pay you interest for the privilege of using your money. Keep in mind that the borrower's ability to honor that promise may depend on its strength, resources, and financial performance; and whether your investment is insured.

Bonds

A bond, often purchased by investors to generate income, is basically an IOU sold by the government or a company in order to raise money. In return for the loan, the bond investor is promised a return of the principal plus periodic interest payments—usually twice a year. If you buy a bond on the day it is issued, you can expect a fixed interest income over a certain time period, as well as the return of your principal at the end of the term. This represents *contractual* income that's more reliable than dividend income, because dividends are changed quarterly by a company's board of directors.

Typically, people tend to introduce more bonds into their portfolios as they get closer to retirement, as a way to reduce risk. But it doesn't eliminate risk. The bond market can dip; and though it rarely happens, it's possible for the government or corporation issuing the bond to go into default, meaning it would be unable to pay all your interest payments or repay your principal. It's possible for you to buy a bond with a coupon rate of 5 percent only to see the company fall on hard times and pay you only 3 percent, or be unable to pay back your principal on the agreed upon date. These are rare occurrences, but they do happen.

Whenever interest rates remain low for several years, the media will often say bonds are overvalued, representing a *bubble* ready to burst when interest rates rise, resulting in a drastic drop in their value. But there are pockets in the bond market that can still achieve solid returns even when interest rates rise. Consult your financial advisor to construct a bond-investment strategy that can withstand a bubble burst.

The *term* of a bond is the time period between the initial issue date of the bond and its maturity date. Short-term bonds are those with a term of 1 to 5 years. The term of intermediate-term bonds is 5 to 10 years, and the duration of long-term bonds is more than 10 years. A bond's interest rate, often called a *coupon rate,* is the stated rate of interest on an issued bond. It's usually determined by the length of the term (generally, the longer the term the higher the interest) and the credit of the bond issuer. The creditworthiness of corporate or municipal bonds is rated by independent rating services.

The reason long-term bonds, or those issued by entities with low credit ratings, usually offer higher interest rates is because they carry a higher risk that the issuer will not repay your principal or pay you interest. Conversely, shorter term bonds, or those issued by entities with higher credit ratings, tend to offer lower interest rates but carry lower risk. Think of bonds as behaving like whips. If you grip the handle of a whip and pull downward, the grip moves very little but the end of the whip moves a lot. In the same way, when interest rates fall or rise, short-term bonds don't react with nearly as much volatility as long-term bonds.

Stocks

If you've always wanted to own a business but don't want to start your own, then investing in stocks is the next best thing. Corporations divide their ownership into shares of stock that can be sold. When you buy stock in a corporation, you own part of the business, including any assets such as buildings and inventory. As a part-owner, you can vote on the company's decisions, such as electing the board of directors or opting to merge with another company. The more shares of stock you own, the greater your decision-making clout.

Many people like investing in *common stocks*—securities that represent a portion of ownership in a corporation—because you can buy and sell them quickly without penalty and because their price can shoot skyward if the company performs well.

Though stocks are not a sure thing, they historically have appreciated faster than inflation; and some stocks will also pay you dividends from the company's earnings. The downside to owning stocks is that, unlike cash investments, your investment is not secured by the FDIC or any other agency; and unlike bonds, there is no promise that your initial investment principal will be repaid or that you'll receive any dividends.

PUBLICLY TRADED STOCKS

Though companies can be privately held or publicly traded, this chapter will focus only on publicly traded stock – the kind that anyone can buy. Company's offer two classes of such stocks—*common stock* and *preferred stock*. Common and preferred stock are mutually exclusive, meaning you can own common shares, preferred shares, or both—but they are distinct types of ownership in a company.

Most publicly traded shares are common stock, which provide the owner with a greater potential for share price appreciation than preferred stock, as well as voting rights that allow the owner to directly participate in the success or failure of the company. This is the kind of stock most of us own. But there's a potential downside. If you own common stock, you are the last in line to receive any of your investment back if the company goes belly up.

Preferred stocks typically offer you greater price stability than common stocks, so they are attractive to investors when the stock market is volatile.

But they have less potential for price appreciation than common stocks and don't allow you any voting rights. Dividends are fixed regardless of how the company performs and are paid before any dividends are paid on common stocks. If the company is unable to pay any dividends, it will repay them to preferred stock holders before any dividends are paid to common stock holders. If the company goes out of business, preferred stock holders will receive a portion of their investment back after creditors and bondholders get their share, but before common stock holders get theirs.

STOCK LINGO

It helps to have at least a working knowledge of common stock terms, so you won't think *bull* is a two-horned mammal and *split* is something to dread at the bowling alley. Here are some short definitions of the most oft-used stock terms:

- *Bull and bear.* A bull market refers to a period of rising stock prices, and a bull is a market optimist who helps drive stock prices up by buying shares. A bear market refers to periods in which stock prices fall (usually by 15 percent or more), and a bear is a market pessimist who sells stocks as prices plummet. The good news is that bull markets historically last longer than bear markets, but informed investors can achieve profits during both bearish and bullish markets.
- *Stock split.* If you hear that your stock has split, there's no need to panic. A stock split occurs when a company decides to divide each share into two or more shares. If, for example, a stock priced at $100 per share splits 2-for-1, it will result in twice as many shares, each worth $50. Though shareholders do not gain or lose any value, stock splits are generally viewed as a positive

occurrence, because they usually occur when the price of a company's shares have become too high to attract new investors. Conversely, a *reverse stock split* occurs when a company reduces the total number of shares, boosting the value of each individual share. Reverse splits rarely occur, but when they do it's viewed as a negative sign.

- *Stock certificates.* A stock certificate proves you own shares in a company. In the past, actual paper certificates were distributed when stock was sold, but nowadays most investors allow the brokerage firm to hold their certificates. If you do take possession of a paper certificate, you must endorse it before delivering it to your broker to sell your stock.

Mutual funds

Mutual funds were first designed in the 1920s to allow people with small amounts of money to own a vast array of securities. Today, mutual funds are the most widely held investment vehicle in America. There are over 8,000 mutual funds in the United States, more than the number of stocks listed on the New York Stock Exchange and American Stock Exchange combined. The popularity is mutual funds stems from the diversification they offer. Most mutual fund portfolios consist of 20 to more than 200 different investments that are managed by the fund's manager, who decides when to buy and sell the investments. When you buy shares in a mutual fund, your money is pooled with the assets of other investors. You can choose to have any profits (distributions) paid to you by check, deposited in your account, or reinvested in the fund. The fund company takes care of all the administrative tasks and provides you with annual or quarterly updates on the fund's performance. Any taxable earnings will be reported to the IRS even if you reinvest them.

MUTUAL FUND PROSPECTUS

But choosing the right mutual fund, or funds, can be a daunting task. Before investing in a mutual fund, it's a good idea to read the fund's *prospectus,* a legal document that includes information about the fund's manager, the fund's objectives and operations, a history of the fund's performance, the fund's top investment holdings, and the types of investments that can be purchased by the fund. We know many of you would rather undergo a root canal that read these rather-lengthy booklets, and you trust that your advisor has read it, so why should you; remember you are being "sold" something so we still advise taking a look at the risk and objective sections, so you have a better understanding of what you where you are placing your hard earned money. Not understanding a fund's objective is one of the most common and costly mistakes we see. If, for example, your fund's objective is to produce income, you can expect there to be some bumps in the road. If the fund's objective is capital preservation, you'll have a steadier ride but one that will probably generate less income. If you wish, your mutual fund company will provide you with a *statement of additional information* upon request.

FUND MANAGER

Because of the vast number of mutual funds, selecting the right fund or funds to invest in can be a challenging enterprise. One of the most important things you should weigh when making that decision is the track record of the fund's manager, the person responsible for making investment decisions with your money. Don't make the mistake of evaluating the past performance of a fund without investigating how long the current manager has been responsible for its performance. And if the manager has recently taken the fund's reins, try to find out what fund he or she previously managed and how it performed during his or her tenure.

To illustrate the enormous importance of investing in a fund headed by a proven manager, consider Jean-Marie Eveillard, in our opinion, one of the greatest fund managers of all time. This Frenchman, currently serving as the senior investment adviser to First Eagle Global, was co-honored in 2001 by Morningstar Inc. as "Stock Manager of the Year" and was a finalist for its 2009 "Fund Manager of the Decade Award" for non-U.S. stocks." In 2003, Morningstar presented him with a "Fund Manager Lifetime Achievement Award." To our point, if you were invested in a Jean-Marie managed fund and he stopped managing the fund, the funds previous track record is that of Jean-Marie, not of the new manager who takes over the fund.

Or David Glancy, who for a decade managed two well known mutual funds—the new Fidelity Leveraged Company and the Fidelity Capital and Income—that both had impressive earnings records. When he left Fidelity in 2003 because his son had become seriously ill, those two funds were ranked among the company's top performers. Glancy managed his own hedge fund firm from his home for a few years until his son recovered. In 2009 Putnam Investments recruited Glancy and put him in charge of its two spectrum funds. Would you rather invest in a mutual fund managed by a 26-year-old still wet behind the ears; or a proven, seasoned and well-respected manager?

MUTUAL FUND FAMILIES

Many mutual fund companies offer an array of funds, referred to as a *family*. Each fund within the family has a different investment objective. If your objectives change, most fund families will allow you to move your money from one fund to another within the family—often at no charge. But it's important to remember that when you make these shifts, you are technically buying and selling funds, so any profits or losses must be reported to the IRS.

A MUTUAL FUND'S NET ASSET VALUE

When you want to check the market value per share of a particular mutual fund, you will typically look in the newspaper or on a website for the term *net asset value*, or *NAV*. The NAV is calculated by subtracting the cost of operations of the fund from the fund's total assets, then dividing that total by the number of shares owned by investors. The NAV for most mutual funds is determined daily after the financial markets close.

MUTUAL FUND CATEGORIES

There are four major categories of mutual funds—*stock funds, hybrid funds, bond funds*, and *money market funds*—each with different objectives, types of investment, and levels of risk. Keep in mind that any one fund might be classified in more than one of these categories:

Stock funds:

- *Small-cap, mid-cap* and *large-cap funds*—named according to the size of the companies in which the fund buys stocks. These funds purchase stocks and their risk varies.
- *Growth funds*—which seek capital appreciation and rarely pay dividends. These funds invest in stocks and carry a high risk.
- *Value funds*—which try to achieve capital appreciation by buying stocks priced low compared to their value and often pay dividends. They invest in stocks and have a medium-high risk.

- *Index fund*—which are designed to mirror the performance of a particular stock index, such as the S&P 500 or the Russell 2000. They generally have lower fees than managed funds and buy stocks that compose a particular market index and their risk varies. They were particularly popular in the 1990s and remain popular today. Although these funds are designed to mirror a particular index, it's important to know you cannot invest directly in an index.

Hybrid funds:

- *Growth and income funds*—which seek to provide long-term capital appreciation and current income. They are medium-risk funds that invest in common and preferred stock, convertible securities, bonds, and money markets.
- *Fixed income funds*—which seek to provide current income and may provide capital appreciation. They invest in bonds and preferred stock, and carry a medium-low risk.
- *Balanced funds*—which are designed to create stability through a balanced portfolio, and they seek to provide income and appreciation. These medium-low risk funds invest in common and preferred stock, bonds, and money markets. You won't hear anyone chattering like a magpie about these funds at your next cocktail party, but they can certainly perform well and be a nice addition to your portfolio.

Bond funds:

- *Corporate funds*—which seek to provide current income. They invest in high-quality corporate bonds, and the risk varies.

- *Government funds*—which attempt to provide current income. These low-risk funds invest in treasury and government agency bonds.
- *Municipal funds*—which seek to provide tax-free income. Income from these funds is federally tax-exempt, but only exempt from state taxes if your fund invests in the state in which you live. Their risk varies, and they invest in state, city or other local government bonds.
- *High-yield funds*—which are sometimes called *junk-bond funds* and attempt to provide high current income. These high-risk funds invest in low-rated corporate or municipal bonds. They've had quite a run in recent years because they have the return profile of stocks, often plus good dividends.

Money market funds:

- *Money market funds* have no potential for capital appreciation but produce income based on current interest rates. These funds carry a very low risk; and invest in the short-term debt of the U.S. government, corporations and banks; they typically maintain a $1 share price, but that is not guaranteed.

Exchange traded funds

An exchange-traded fund is a group of securities that, with a single purchase, provides you with a diversified portfolio. Because ETFs are traded on exchanges like stocks, you can buy and sell them throughout the day if you wish. They try to mimic market indexes or sectors by investing in all or a representative sample of the stocks or bonds in that index or sector.

Exchange traded funds often have low annual management fees, which are disclosed—along with any other charges and expenses—in the prospectus. They are tax efficient and provide you with financial transparency through daily portfolio disclosures. Unlike an actively managed mutual fund that sells securities for gains or to meet shareholders' redemptions, ETFs sell securities to reflect a particular index or sector. The transaction fee to buy or sell an ETF has a minimal impact on larger investments; but a significant impact on smaller, ongoing investments.

Individual investors typically buy shares of an ETF on the secondary market from other investors. An ETF's price is based on supply and demand. ETFs are subject to the same risks as those of the underlying securities. Some ETFs have more risk than others—depending on the risk of the asset subclass the fund is tracking or the trading volume or liquidity of the ETF. Capital gains, interest, or dividends are passed along to you and reported to the IRS. You generally don't pay any capital gains until you sell the fund. It's important for you to know that with an ETF, some brokerage houses will charge you a commission for reinvesting your dividends back into the ETF, so ask the right questions as these charges could significantly reduce your returns overtime.

Unit investment trusts

You can buy a certain number of "units" of a *unit investment trust*, for which investment professionals buy and supervise a portfolio. Each portfolio is either designed to invest in a particular sector or accomplish a stated investment objective—such as growth or income. A specific time period or term is set for the duration of each trust, and the portfolio stays the same over the life of the trust because it is not actively managed. If you hold the trust to maturity, or longer than 12 months, all your capital gains will be taxed at the long-term rate.

Like ETFs, you receive a diversified portfolio with a single investment in a UIT. You can sell your units at any time, either on the secondary market or back to the trust at its current net asset value. You'll receive your share of the trust's earned income, and at maturity you will receive proceeds from the assets of the trust (A prospectus is available for each trust). We like "UIT's" because of the maturity feature of most (usually 15 to 24 months). Imagine if your entire investment account was forced to be sold and now it's in cash; it now forces you to make another decision with those dollars. We have found many investors will buy an investment, but rarely will they sell it. Using a UIT, that has a maturity date, will force that issue.

Individually managed accounts

When you invest in an *individually managed account*, you usually must invest $100,000 or more. You specify your time horizon, risk tolerance, and investment objectives to your professional money manager so he or she can use that information to construct and actively manage for you a customized portfolio. Because you own each investment in the portfolio directly, meaning you don't pool your money with other investors unless you own mutual funds within the managed account, your account is not affected by the actions of other investors using the same portfolio manager. You pay taxes only on the capital gains you actually realize, and your money manager can buy tax-exempt investments or use tax management strategies to minimize your tax liability.

Your money manager typically will charge you 1 to 2 percent to manage your account in a manner that is directly in line with your personal goals and objectives. When you invest in a mutual fund, you simply put your money in and allow the fund's manager to make buying and selling decisions based on certain rules and his or her personal insights. But with an individually managed account, you sit down with a money manager and say things like, "I'm a growth and income investor," or "I need this amount of income each month from my investments," and the manager will make investment decisions within those parameters.

Tax-deferred annuities

Some people enjoy giving annuities a bad rap, but as David often says, "Don't be down on something you're not up on." Many people invest in *tax-deferred annuities* in order to provide them with retirement income, defer taxes, or avoid probate. These annuities allow you to accumulate assets tax-deferred to provide you with future income, though the tax-deferral is not allowed for corporate or trust-owned policies. You can make withdrawals during the deferral period, but a penalty might apply to withdrawals prior to age 59½. Tax-deferred annuities can be annuitized to begin lifetime income payments, but that guarantee is subject to the claims-paying ability of the insurance company issuing the payments. You can avoid probate if your death occurs prior to the contract's annuitization, because the funds are directed by a beneficiary form. All annuities are issued by insurance companies, so it's important to know the claims paying ability of the insurance company you have invested with, and are not guaranteed by the FDIC or any other government agency.

We will discuss four types of tax-deferred annuities—*fixed, fixed indexed, variable and immediate annuities.*

FIXED ANNUITIES

A fixed annuity is similar to a time deposit at your bank. It will normally have a fixed interest rate for a specified period on time and will have a set maturity date. As an example you might see a 5 year fixed annuity, paying 3%. If you invest $100,000, you will earn $3000 a year until the fifth year at which time it matures. Most insurance companies will allow you to renew the contract, but at a different rate, similar to the way a time deposit would reset at maturity. The predictable nature of a fixed annuity is one reason it's a popular option for many retirees who want a known income stream to supplement their other retirement income.

FIXED INDEX ANNUITIES

Most Fixed Indexed Annuities are long-term investments and are used during the accumulation phase your life; some offer income and death benefits similar to a variable annuity (which you will read about next), but all offer participation in market indices with a principal guarantee and most will reset the index values annually. INVESTOPEDIA explains an 'Indexed Annuity' this way: Insurance companies commonly offer a provision of a guaranteed minimum return with indexed annuities, so even if the stock index does poorly, the annuitant will have some of his downside risk of loss limited. However, it also is common for an annuitant's yields to be somewhat lower than expected due to the combination of caps on the maximum amount of interest earned and fee-related deductions.

For example, suppose an indexed annuity is based on the S&P 500, which earns 10% one year. The terms of an indexed annuity state that fees will be 2.5% and that the maximum cap on returns is 9%. In this case, the annuitant would only receive a total of 6.5% (9%-2.5%) return from his or her annuity. Like most annuities, if surrendered early it will likely be subject to hefty surrender charges.

VARIABLE ANNUITIES

A variable annuity is a long-term financial vehicle that's basically a contractual agreement in which you make payments to an insurance company, which then agrees to pay you an income or a lump sum amount at a later date. There are contract limitations, fees, and charges associated with variable annuities. Annual expenses could exceed 3.5 percent per year. Early withdrawals from a variable annuity may be subject to surrender charges and taxed as ordinary income. And when you make withdrawals from a variable annuity, it reduces the annuity contract benefits and values.

If you invest in a variable annuity, you put up a lump sum, say $100,000, which is then invested in various sub accounts that will rise or fall in concert with the fluctuations of the market, minus costs. After a number of years, you can make withdrawals from this account in a lump sum or periodic payments, just as you would from most other investments. When you make the withdrawals they may be less than the original amount you invested.

Why would you buy an investment that can go up and down with the markets, take money out like most other investments, but pay higher fees for it? Two reasons, guaranteed income or death benefit protection.

If you pay for income protection or death benefit protection, the insurance company promises to credit your original investment with a fixed increase—5 percent for example—every year, plus a higher dollar amount if your investments do well. Even if your investments perform poorly, the minimum guaranteed increase is still honored. You *can't* take that increase in value in a lump sum, but you can take it out in payments for the rest of your life. See the prospectus for details.

Let's say you have a $100,000 variable annuity with a 5 percent income guarantee, but the stock market plunges, reducing the worth of your investment to $70,000. But because your guaranteed income account has still been credited with 5 percent compounded annually on the original $100,000, it would be worth about $163,000. So if you held onto the annuity for 10 years, you could turn it into $8,150 a year for life. Each contract is different, as to when you can access a life time income stream, so again read the details in the prospectus.

As far as death benefits are concerned – using our example above, if you $100,000 investment was worth $70,000 when you die and you had elected for a "return of premium death benefit" your heirs would receive $100,000 not the current value of $70,000. Many insurance companies will offer enhanced death benefit options (at a cost), which may capture the highest anniversary value or increase annually at a fixed percentage. The goals and objectives you have for your money should determine if a variable annuity is right for you.

One way to put the additional cost of a variable annuity into perspective is to illustrate it, using Cruise Ships as an example. Doug is a Cruise enthusiast and when I (David) posed this question to Doug recently we both thought "what a great way to illustrate the cost of variable annuity". There are two cruises you are contemplating taking, both have the same itineraries, ports of call, food and entertainment selection and the ships are identical, except for one thing…one ship has life boats and the other doesn't. The cruise for the ship that has no life boats cost $2000 for the trip; the cost of the cruise with the life boats is $2300. The question is "are you willing to pay the extra $300 for the life boats"? With a variable annuity the life boat is your income and death benefits. Some say yes, others say no; the decision is really up to you if it's worth the extra cost.

IMMEDIATE ANNUITIES

There are two main types of immediate annuities—an *immediate fixed annuity* in which you put up a sum of money and the insurance company pays you a fixed number of dollars per month for the rest of your life or for the term you choose; and an *immediate variable annuity* in which your money is invested in a mix of stock and bond mutual funds, and the insurer pays you a monthly fixed percentage of the portfolio's value, which could rise and fall. With both types, you can choose a beneficiary, who would receive your payments should you die. You generally will get a larger initial payout from the immediate fixed annuity, but the immediate variable annuity's payments might increase over time.

Let's say you put $100,000 in a 10-year immediate fixed annuity that pays you $7,000 a year. That's a fairly nice income stream. If you die in Year 6, for example, you beneficiary would receive $7,000 a year for the remaining four years. Because you will not get your principal back when you die or when the term of the annuity expires, this is may not be a good investment option if you are concerned about leaving a tidy sum to your heirs. Think of an immediate annuity this way; you are exchanging cash for cash flow.

ANNUITY WITHDRAWALS

When you are ready to begin withdrawing money from an annuity, you have several choices. For *non-annuitized* withdrawals, taxation is based on a last-in, first-put method. Any increase in value is taxed before the return of principal. Also, surrender charges, withdrawal charges, and tax penalties may apply. For *annuitized* withdrawals, a portion of each annuitized withdrawal is considered a tax-free return of principal until the initial investment has been fully recovered. Future withdrawals are then taxed as ordinary income.

Before buying an annuity you should talk to a financial professional, because you don't want to make a mistake that will cost you or your beneficiary. With a non-annuitized annuity, you can either take a lump sum of money or make systematic withdrawals. But with an annuitized annuity, you have various options—such as receiving payouts for life or over a specific period of years, having those payouts go only to you, or having the payouts or part of those payments go to your beneficiary when you die. A lot of people make the mistake of opting for *single life* benefit, then die a few years later and leave their spouse or other beneficiary with no income from the annuity. If you choose the *joint and survivor* benefit, your beneficiary will get all or a percentage of your benefit.

Common investment risks

With investments, as it is in life, there is always some risk. Don't make the mistake of thinking about risk simply in terms of potentially losing some or your entire principal. There are at least seven major types of risk, and regardless of how hard you try, it's impossible to avoid them all.

MARKET RISK

Market risk is the potential that an investment will fall in price if its particular financial market performs poorly. For example, if you're local real estate market drops, most homes and commercial real estate in that market will decrease in price. Or if the general stock market takes a dive, the price of most stocks will also fall.

BUSINESS RISK

Business risk is the possibility that an investment will decrease in value due to issues such as unsuccessful products, labor problems, or poor financial performance. If, for example, a business is performing poorly, its stock may decrease in price or even become worthless. Or if a company can't repay its obligations, it may default on its bonds.

INTEREST RATE RISK

Interest rate risk is the potential for escalating interest rates to cause an investment to fall in price. For example, when interest rates go up, the current market price of bonds goes down and the performance of stocks generally falls—especially if they have a large amount of debt.

INFLATION RISK

Inflation risk is the chances that that an investment will fail to keep up with inflation, which may result in very conservative investors slowly going broke as they steadily lose purchasing power. Those who invest only in certificates of deposit or bonds held to maturity will hang onto their principal and earn a paltry interest rate, but will see their purchasing power gradually vanish into thin air.

LIQUIDITY RISK

Liquidity risk, also known as marketability risk, is the potential that an investment cannot be sold quickly for a reasonable price. If you have to sell some real estate in a hurry and can't wait patiently for a good offer to come your way, you may have to settle for less-than-market value. If you have to sell a CD before it matures, you will incur a penalty.

OPPORTUNITY RISK

Opportunity risk is the perceived loss you incur when your assets are currently tied up in an investment, making them unavailable to earn a higher rate of return through some other investment. This lost opportunity is called *opportunity cost*. For example, if you have money tied up in a CD or bond when interest rates rise or the stock market begins to perform well, you will incur an opportunity cost by missing out on those potential gains. Likewise, if one of your stocks or mutual funds doesn't perform well, you've not only suffered an unrealized loss, but have lost money on the interest you would have earned on your full principal if you'd been invested in a bond or CD.

CURRENCY RISK

Currency risk comes with any investments you might have outside the United States. If you sell foreign assets—such as international mutual funds—when the value of the dollar is up, you will receive less money due to the exchange rate alone.

Risk management strategies

As we said earlier, there is no way to eliminate all forms of risk from your investments. If you're a conservative investor who puts all your money into savings accounts, you'll face no market, business or interest rate risk, but you will face inflation risk. If you're a little more adventurous and invest in bonds, you'll face some market and interest rate risk, but you will encounter business risk and possibly inflation risk. That being said, there are some ways to manage many of the risks associated with investing, but none of these will eliminate the possibility of loss.

DOLLAR COST AVERAGING

If you're allowing your employer to take a set amount from your paycheck and invest it in your 401(k), then you are already dollar cost averaging. Dollar cost averaging is a risk-management technique in which you put a set amount of money every month into a stock or mutual fund, enabling you to buy more shares of the investment when the price is lower but fewer shares when the price is higher. This strategy will reduce your market risk, but it won't guarantee you a profit on your investments or protect you against loss in a declining market.

STAGGER FIXED-INCOME MATURITIES

By staggering the maturity dates of fixed-income securities (such as bonds), you can allow your investments to mature and be reinvested at different times at various interest rates, thus reducing your interest rate risk.

DIVERSIFICATION

You can use diversification to reduce both your inflation risk and business risk. This technique involves putting money in several different investments as opposed to a single investment, ensuring that if some of your investments don't perform well, they will be offset by others that perform above average.

To illustrate how diversification can produce a greater return on your investment, let's consider Jim and Jenni—each of whom makes an initial investment of $50,000. Jim puts all his money in a single investment that earns 6 percent per year. Jenni, who's more of a risk taker, makes five different investments of $10,000 each. At the end of 20 years, Jim's investment has grown to $165,510. Jenni loses all her principal from one of her $10,000 investments, but with her other four $10,000 investments earns 2 percent, 4 percent, 8 percent and 12 percent respectively. At the end of 20 years Jenni's investments have grown to $195,333—nearly $30,000 more than Jim's. Her's was a smoother ride to a higher place.

ASSET ALLOCATION

Asset allocation is the process of diversifying your portfolio among several different asset classes for the purpose of reducing your risk and increasing your returns. Though the technique is simple in concept, it can be difficult to implement. You should consult a qualified financial advisor to help you develop an asset allocation that meets your needs and objectives.

> "You have life insurance for one of two reasons—
> either you owe someone or you love someone."
> -David Hays

7

INSURANCE, RISK MANAGEMENT AND ASSET PROTECTION

If you save and invest your money for many years, it's likely that by the time you near retirement you will have accumulated a sizeable stash of assets. Needless to say, suffering a major financial loss at that critical juncture, or later during retirement, could be devastating.

To avoid such a crippling setback, you need to manage life's risks and protect your assets by such things as life insurance, health insurance, long-term care insurance, and disability income insurance—not to mention Medicare or Medicaid.

We strongly recommend that, just prior to retiring, you sit down with a financial professional and conduct a comprehensive review of your insurance coverage. Some have the mistaken notion that buying insurance is a waste of money, while in reality it's a way to transfer risk from you to the insurance company. If you incur a financial loss of some sort, the insurance company will reimburse you based on your coverage. Even if you never suffer a loss, and we hope you don't, insurance provides you and your family with something that's hard to put a price tag on—peace of mind.

Property and casualty insurance

There are four basic types of property and casualty insurance, which we will briefly describe:

AUTOMOBILE INSURANCE

This insurance is fairly expensive, due to the high frequency of accidents and claims. You are legally required to have liability coverage that insures you, your passengers, and the drivers of other vehicles and their automobiles. You may also choose to obtain full coverage that insures your automobile.

HOMEOWNER'S INSURANCE

Homeowner's insurance insures not only your house, but your personal property and liability claims for medical expenses if someone is injured while on your property. You can buy additional coverage for damage or loss as a result of a flood or earthquake, or to insure expensive items such as jewelry or business equipment.

RENTER'S INSURANCE

If you rent, your personal belongings are not covered by your landlord's insurance. That's why you need to buy renter's insurance, which covers your personal property from damage or loss as a result of such things as fire, theft, or vandalism. Like homeowner's insurance, you can buy additional coverage for damage or loss as a result of flood or earthquake, or to insure expensive items you own.

UMBRELLA LIABILITY INSURANCE

If you wish, you can purchase an umbrella liability policy to supplement the coverage in your auto and homeowner's policies. It provides additional liability coverage that begins where your other personal liability policy coverage ends. It's quite inexpensive, but can protect you from a lawsuit that could slam you with a financial loss of staggering proportions. Some umbrella policies even pay for legal expenses and liabilities not covered under your auto or homeowner's policies.

Disability income insurance

It's important that you don't take for granted one of your greatest financial assets—your ability to earn a living. If this asset is snatched away by a debilitating illness or injury, you might incur medical expenses not covered by your health insurance plan, and might even permanently lose your ability to work.

You may have a false sense of security because you have worker's compensation, but this only provides you with protection if your injury is caused by an accident at work. You may feel you're protected by Social Security, but that program's disability benefits are provided only if you can't work at all for at least 12 months, and then you must wait six more months to receive your first benefit check.

The most effective way to protect your ability to produce income is with disability insurance. If you become disabled, your policy will pay you a percentage of your wages. That benefit can not only help you pay your medical expenses, but enable you to maintain your lifestyle—even if you lose your salary.

There are four basic types of disability insurance:

- Group disability insurance—usually offered through your employer as an employee benefit. Some employers pay a portion of the premiums.
- Individual disability insurance—offered by insurance companies directly to individuals. This insurance is often purchased when a group policy is not available, or as a supplement to group coverage.
- Short-term disability insurance. This group or individual coverage often covers disabilities lasting 13 or 26 weeks, though coverage may last for as long as two years.
- Long-term disability insurance. This group or individual coverage provides extended disability benefits that might last for the length of the disability, until age 65, or for life.

QUESTIONS TO ASK

If you're obtaining disability insurance coverage through your employer's group plan, you may not have many choices. Nonetheless, it's important that you unearth the answers to several key questions, such as:

- Am I buying a short-term or long-term policy?
- What is the policy's *waiting period*—the period of time from the beginning of your disability until you begin to receive disability insurance benefits? It's usually less than a month for short-term policies and three-to-six months for long-term policies.

- How long is the *benefit period*, the period of time that your monthly disability benefits (often a percentage of your salary) will last?
- Will I be taxed on my disability benefit payments?
- Can my premiums be raised?
- Can my policy be cancelled?
- Am I covered if I'm unable to work in my profession or perform any type of work?
- What is the financial strength of the company issuing my policy?

Health insurance

A serious illness has the potential to savage your retirement savings with a two-edged sword—costly medical expenses and the loss of your ability to earn a living. Having sufficient health insurance coverage can help you cope with half of that two-pronged problem by paying for a significant portion of your medical bills and related expenses.

You have two basic options—a *group plan* usually offered by companies as an employee benefit, or an *individual policy* offered by insurance companies directly to an individual or family:

- Group plan—Your employer might pay for a portion of your premiums, and often will offer insurance coverage for your family members for an additional premium.
- Individual policy—This is usually purchased by people who don't have access to a group policy or Medicare coverage. Its cost often depends on such factors as the type of policy, deductibles, benefit limits, and the age and health history of the individual and/or family members.

NEW COVERAGE OPTIONS

Under the Affordable Care Act, a *pre-existing condition insurance plan* is now available to those with a pre-existing health condition who have been uninsured for at least six months, or have previously been denied coverage because of their health problem. States can run this new insurance plan themselves, or ask the Department of Health and Human Services to establish a plan for them. For more information about pre-existing condition insurance plan visit www.healthcare.gov.

Medicare

Medicare is a health insurance program provided by the federal government. You become eligible for Medicare at the beginning of the month you turn 65, or earlier if you become permanently disabled. There are four types of coverage provided by Medicare, labeled by letters A through D:

- Medicare Part A—This coverage helps cover the costs of hospital care, rehab care at a nursing home, hospice care, and limited home health care. It financed by Medicare payroll taxes paid by employees and employers, and a trust fund in which surpluses are deposited.
- Medicare Part B—This helps cover the costs of doctors' bills, outpatient and emergency room services, ambulance services, diagnostic tests, laboratory services, and medical equipment such as wheelchairs and walkers. It's financed by general tax revenues and premiums collected from participants in the plan.
- Medicare Part C—Participants in Medicare Part A and B are eligible for expanded-care plans (such as an HMO or PPO)

run by Medicare-approved, private insurance companies. These plans are called Medicare Advantage plans, and most of them also offer prescription drug coverage.
- Medicare Part D—Those receiving Medicare Part A and/or Part B are eligible for the voluntary Part D program. They can choose from a number of plans offered by private companies that cover prescription drugs, subject to co-payments and deductibles.

MEDICARE INSURANCE PREMIUMS

With Medicare Part C and Medicare Part D, your premiums will vary depending on which plan you select. With Medicare Part B, there is a standard monthly premium that changes each year, but you may have to pay more than that if your modified adjusted gross income exceeds a certain limit that also varies each year.

If you enroll in Medicare Part D and your income exceeds the same threshold that applies to Medicare Part B, you'll have to pay an income-related monthly adjustment amount in addition to your Part D premium. With Medicare Part A, your premium will be determined in the same way as your Social Security benefits—by the number of qualifying quarters you've amassed in Medicare-covered employment—and it could range from zero to several hundred dollars a month.

MEDICARE TRENDS

Since 2008, the Federal Hospital Insurance Trust Fund that finances Medicare Part A began using interest earnings and asset redemptions to cover the amount of expenditures that exceeded tax income. If the fund continues to follow this path, it is projected to become exhausted in 2024. The Federal Supplementary Medical Insurance Trust Fund that finances Medicare Parts B and D is sufficiently financed for at least the next decade, because premium and general revenue income for Parts B and D are reset each year to match expected costs.

Long-Term Care

Before we address the importance of long-term care insurance, we need to define long-term care. Basically, it's either *personal care* or *skilled care*. Personal care includes helping a person with daily living activities such as eating, bathing, using the restroom, and moving from place to place. Skilled care is medical care given to a person by licensed professionals—such as nurses, therapists, and physicians.

Long-term care might be necessary if you develop a disability, cognitive impairment, or chronic physical condition or illness. You can receive the care in your home, the community, an assisted-living facility, or a nursing home. Unlike medical and hospital care, most long-term care is not designed to cure your medical conditions, but to manage them.

About 70 percent of Americans who live to the age of retirement will need long-term care services at some point in their lives, [27] and the lifetime probability of people age 65 or older becoming disabled in at least two activities of daily living, or of being cognitively impaired, is 68 percent. [28] Forty-two percent of people in need of long-term care are 64 years of age or younger. [29] Because women in general have longer life

---

[27] 2013 Long-Term Care Planning Handbook, Federal Handbooks Inc.
[28] AARP Beyond 50," a 2003 report on Independent Living and Disability.
[29] Analysis by the Healthy Policy Institute, Georgetown University, of data from the 2005 National Health Interview Survey and 2004 National Nursing Home Survey.

expectancies than men, they are more likely to eventually need long-term care.

HOW PEOPLE PAY FOR LONG-TERM CARE

While the cost of long-term care depends on factors such as where you live and the type of care you receive, the cost of long-term care has been rising for years, and is expected to continue climbing upward in the future. The average annual cost of long-term care in 2013 was $81,030 to $90,520 for nursing home care, $42,600 for assisted living care, and $30,660 for home health care.[30]

So how do people pay for such pricey services? Some pay for it themselves, or ask family members to foot the bill. Most rely on Medicaid, the only government program that pays for long-term nursing home care. In fact, nearly 62 percent of long-term care expenditures in the U.S. are paid by Medicaid funds.[31] But here's the catch. You have to be virtually broke before Medicaid kicks in, because this federal/state program is based on need. The federal government sets Medicaid guidelines and individual states make rules, so Medicaid programs differ from state to state.

WHO QUALIFIES?

A nursing home patient is not allowed to have more than a certain dollar amount of *countable assets*— things like bank accounts, certificates of deposit, stocks, bonds, annuities, and more than one automobile—and still qualify for Medicaid. The patient's spouse living at home is allowed to keep a limited amount of countable assets to live on. The dollar limits for the patient and spouse vary from state to state. Most states offer a

---

[30] 2012 Met Life Survey

[31] 2011 National Health Policy Forum.

Long-Term Care Partnership Program that allows people qualifying for Medicaid to keep $1 of assets for every $1 paid out by a qualifying long-term care policy. The program's requirements vary from state to state.

To qualify for Medicaid, there are also income limits that vary from state to state, as well as a *look-back period*—the five-year period immediately preceding a person's application for nursing home Medicaid benefits. Any gifts the person makes during this period affects the person's eligibility for Medicaid. The amount of the gift divided by the average monthly private-pay cost of nursing home care in the person's home state will equal the *penalty period*—the number of months the person is ineligible for Medicaid. But gifts to certain recipients may not trigger a period of Medicaid ineligibility.

WILL MEDICARE PAY FOR LONG-TERM CARE?

Medicare will not pay for long-term care. This federal health insurance program covers short-term skilled care, such as rehabilitation therapy received in a nursing home. But unless you're receiving hospice care, your injury or illness must be improving in order for you to continue receiving Medicare benefits. And because Medicare's shaky long-term solvency will force the government to make some changes to the program, there is no guarantee that today's Medicare benefits will be available in the future.

Long-Term Care Insurance

We feel one of the most commonly overlooked retirement planning issues is *long-term care insurance,* insurance that provides you coverage for long-term skilled medical care provided in such places as a nursing home, assisted living facility, or your home. Because these kinds of care usually cost tens of thousands of dollars a year, long-term care insurance helps protect your assets, preserve your sense of self-sufficiency by not relying on family members to pay for your care, and give you more options when choosing the type of care and the quality of care you will receive.

When you buy a long-term care insurance policy, you are transferring the risk of paying for long-term care from yourself to the insurance company. Because long-term care insurance policies are expensive, those with low incomes and few assets are usually unable to afford the premiums. But one nice thing about long-term care policies is that the policy premiums can usually be deducted on your federal tax return, and you may also get a tax break on your state taxes as well. What's more, if you cancel your disability insurance and no longer have to pay those premiums, it will free up some money to help pay for your long-term care policy.

Some people choose to acquire long-term care insurance by combining long-term care coverage with an annuity or life insurance policy. If you make withdrawals from one of these *combination* policies to pay for long-term care, the withdrawals are not taxable. In a life insurance/long term care combination policy, the long-term care insurance is usually added in the form of a rider on the permanent life policy, and any amount used to pay for long-term care is subtracted from the death benefit.

WHEN SHOULD YOU BUY IT?

Though some experts recommend buying long-term care insurance at around age 55, we feel a good rule of thumb is to buy it before you need it, and while you're still healthy enough to qualify for coverage. About 40 percent of people who need long-term care are ages 18 to 64.[32] In general, the younger you are when you buy the insurance, the lower your premium will be.

WHEN WILL BENEFITS BEGIN?

Before providing long-term care benefits, most policies require that you can no longer perform two or more *activities of daily living*—such as bathing, feeding, and dressing yourself. These ADLs vary from policy to policy, but a significant cognitive impairment alone is usually enough to trigger the flow of benefits.

PICKING THE RIGHT PLAN

When selecting a long-term care policy, it's a good idea to buy it from an insurance company that's been around for many years, has a proven track record of financial strength and stability, and has a solid credit rating. Insurance company credit ratings are provided by companies such as AM Best, Standard & Poor's, Moody's, and Weiss Ratings.

You might wish to take advantage of group long-term care insurance if it's offered by your employer as an employee benefit. But before signing up be sure to compare the post-employment price of group coverage with individual policy coverage, and make sure your rates won't increase if you leave the company. When comparing a group plan with an individual plan, be aware that some individual policies will offer a discount if both spouses purchase a policy.

---

[32] 2013 Long-Term Care Planning Handbook, Federal Handbooks Inc.

OTHER FACTORS TO CONSIDER

In general, the greater coverage provided in a long-term care policy, the higher your premiums will be. Your monthly benefits will generally range from $1,000 to $7,000 a month, but lifetime coverage caps may apply. Before buying a policy, here are some things to check:

- *Alzheimer's coverage.* While most policies cover mental impairment as defined by the policy, not all cover diseases such as Alzheimer's disease.
- *Home health care and assisted living care.* Some policies provide benefit payments for home health care and assisted living care in addition to nursing home care.
- *Length of coverage.* The common length of coverage—the amount of time your policy will pay benefits—is three to four years. But to ensure you never need to rely upon Medicaid, you should consider longer coverage.
- *Waiting period.* This period, also called the elimination period, specifies the length of time between the beginning of your long-term care and the time when your benefits begin. A common waiting period is 100 days.
- *Pre-existing condition.* Most policies specify a period of time—usually six months—before the policy will pay benefits for pre-existing conditions.
- *Guaranteed renewable.* A guaranteed renewable policy means the insurance company cannot cancel your policy as long as you pay the premiums. Insurance companies are not allowed to hike long-term care insurance premiums on individual policyholders, but with state approval can raise rates across the board on a defined group of policyholders who have the same type of policy.

- *Inflation rider.* A policy with an inflation rider provides you with inflation protection by raising your benefits by a certain percentage—often 5 percent—per year.
- *Waiver of premium.* This policy feature eliminates premium payments during the time you are receiving benefit payments.
- *No forfeiture.* This feature enables you to cancel your policy, but still receive reduced benefits if you require long-term care.
- *Tax qualified.* Benefits from a tax-qualified policy—one that meets federal requirements and covers qualified care services needed by chronically-ill patients—are not subject to federal tax.
- *Policy exclusions.* Some policies don't cover such things as care received outside the U.S.; or care resulting from anxiety, depression, or substance abuse.

LAST-DITCH MEASURES

If you or your parents do not have long-term care insurance, you can take some emergency measures, especially near the end of life, to pay for long-term care, such as:

- Access the cash value of your life insurance policy by canceling it or taking a loan against it. Be aware that if you cancel your current policy, you may not be eligible to buy another policy; and if you take a loan against your policy it will reduce the death benefit.
- If your life insurance policy has a provision for living benefits or accelerated death benefits, you may begin receiving benefits while you are alive (subject to restrictions). You normally must have a short life expectancy to qualify for this provision.

- Through a *viatical settlement*, you can sell your life insurance policy for a lump sum to a company that becomes the beneficiary. These settlements are generally available only to people with a short life expectancy, and are not subject to income tax if used for nursing home care.

Life insurance

You buy most types of insurance—to cover such things as your car, home, or health care needs—with the hope that you never need to use them. But with life insurance, the question is not *if* you will need to use the benefit, but *when*. Many policies now offer a critical illness rider, where the benefit can be accelerated for things such as long-term care.

There are two main types of life insurance—*term insurance*, which is purchased for a specific period of time and provides a death benefit only if you die during that time span; and *cash value insurance*, in which part of your premium is deposited into a cash reserve and the remainder is used to pay for a death benefit.

All types of life insurance charge you a premium in return for the promise to pay your beneficiaries a death benefit when you pass away. The cost of life insurance varies—depending on your gender, age, and health; and the type of insurance and amount of coverage you select. Life insurance has a favorable and unique tax treatment that can be used to create a more effective financial plan.

Life insurance can provide *death benefits* that can preserve your dependents' standard of living, eliminate home mortgage or loan balances, provide a charitable gift, or create an immediate estate. Life insurance can also provide *living benefits* that can be used to create a cash reserve, provide additional retirement income, maximize your pension income, or pay for long-term or hospice care.

Life insurance should be a cornerstone of your financial plan. Without it, your family members may not have the resources to meet their financial needs. It will be difficult enough for your loved ones to cope with your death without facing additional financial burdens resulting from your lack of having a life insurance policy.

PICKING THE RIGHT PLAN

Because selecting the type and amount of life insurance coverage to meet your current and future needs can be difficult, it's a good idea to consult your financial professional, who can help you make an informed decision and explain which coverage best fits into your overall financial plan.

Unfortunately, there is no standard rule of thumb to use when determining which type of life insurance is right for you and the amount of coverage you need. Some of the factors to consider are your financial obligations and lifestyle; estate considerations; and the age, income and assets of you and your dependents.

Making the matter even murkier is the fact that your life insurance needs will likely change over time. For example, depending on your personal and financial situations, you may find that your life insurance needs decrease when you retire. It's a good idea to have your life insurance coverage reviewed by a seasoned professional from time to time, especially when you experience a major life change. Many newer life policies offer the flexibility to access a portion of the death benefit to pay for the cost of long-term care.

TERM INSURANCE

Term insurance premiums, particularly at first, are usually less expensive than cash value insurance premiums. But if you are still living when the policy expires, neither you nor your beneficiaries will receive any benefits. It may be the right choice for you if you need death benefit coverage only for a certain period of time, can't afford a higher premium payment, or have no need to accumulate cash value or borrow against your policy. Because term life may have significantly lower premiums, disciplined investors may want to buy term insurance and invest the difference.

There are three main types of term insurance:

- *Level Premium*—in which the death benefit and premium payments remain the same for the entire term of the policy.
- *Annual Renewable*—in which the policy may be renewed each year, usually at a higher premium due to your increasing risk of dying. But your death benefit remains the same.
- *Decreasing Term*—in which your premiums remain the same, but your death benefit decreases each year.

CASH VALUE INSURANCE

Cash value policies are often referred to as *permanent* insurance. The premiums during the first several years are usually more expensive than comparable term policies. However, the payments may be lower, and the benefits may be greater, than comparable term coverage over the lifetime of the policy. In a cash value policy, part of the premium pays for a death benefit, while the remainder is deposited into a cash reserve. If you die while covered under the policy, your beneficiaries will receive a death benefit, but you can access the policy's cash value while you're still living.

Cash value insurance might be a good choice for you if you want or need long-term life insurance coverage, are seeking to accumulate cash value in the policy on a tax-deferred basis, and (unlike 401ks and IRAs) don't want required minimum distributions or age restrictions for your contributions. Here are some other reasons why you might want to opt for cash value insurance:

- You want to (unlike 401ks, IRAs and Roth IRAs) avoid contribution limits. But additional cash value contributions can't be made to *whole life* or *variable life* insurance policies, and maximum contribution limits might apply to some *universal life* and variable life policies.
- You want the ability to (unlike 401ks, IRAs, and Roth IRAs) withdraw the cash value tax-free. But remember that partial withdrawals will lower the death benefit by the amount withdrawn, and you'll owe income taxes on the total withdrawals that exceed what's been paid into the policy. Withdrawals are not permitted from whole life insurance policies, and percentage limits apply to withdrawals from *variable universal life* insurance policies.
- You feel you may need to borrow against your policy. Keep in mind that interest payments are usually required for policy loans, and outstanding policy loans at the time of your death will reduce the policy's death benefits.
- You don't want your beneficiary to pay taxes on investment earnings due to a tax-free death benefit. Though the death benefit is usually tax-free, your policy must be held until you die to avoid paying any taxes on investment earnings.

TYPES OF CASH VALUE INSURANCE

There are four main types of cash value insurance:

WHOLE LIFE INSURANCE

This type of cash value insurance guarantees level premiums. If you pay your premiums as specified in your policy, your coverage will remain in effect until you pass away, at which time your beneficiaries will receive a guaranteed death benefit. You will accumulate cash reserves that have minimum guarantee cash values, but you won't be able to control how your money is invested.

UNIVERSAL LIFE

This type of policy offers flexible premiums and an adjustable death benefit. Your premiums are deposited into your cash value account, from which insurance protection and other policy charges are paid. You can deposit additional payments in order to build your cash value more rapidly, and you generally receive a guaranteed interest plus any additional interest on your cash value, which is re-deposited over time. If your cash value is large enough, you can lower your premiums by using that cash value to cover charges, but if your cash value is too low to cover charges, you'll have to pay additional premiums.

INDEX UNIVERSAL LIFE

Index universal life allows the cash value of your policy to be invested in market indexes without the fear of loss. The amount you earn is generally capped, but will not lose value due to changes in the equity or fixed income markets. You will still see a possible decrease in your cash value, due to the cost of insurance being removed from your policy.

The crediting methods are not in the market, but simply tied to the markets. Using a financial professional is important when making the correct policy choice.

VARIABLE LIFE

Variable life is growth-oriented insurance that allows you to decide how to invest your cash value, which may fluctuate based on the performance of your investment selections. You can select from the investment sub-accounts available through the insurance company—such as equity, fixed-income or money market portfolios. While the insurance company guarantees level premiums and a minimum death benefit, your death benefit will increase if your cash value grows.

VARIABLE UNIVERSAL LIFE

This type of insurance provides the investment choices of variable life plus the flexible premiums of universal life. It enables you to determine how much of your premium will be allocated to insurance costs and cash values, and allows you to make additional payments that will be credited to your cash value account. The performance of your investments will determine both your cash value and your death benefit, neither of which is guaranteed.

SURVIVORSHIP LIFE

This type of life insurance policy insures the lives of two people and is available as whole life, universal life, variable life, or variable universal life. Premiums for survivorship life insurance are often less expensive than they would be for two separate policies, since the death benefit is payable only upon the second death. This insurance is not designed to meet the needs of the surviving spouse. Rather, it's often used to pay estate taxes or provide an inheritance.

"Fair isn't always equal"
-David Hays

8

ESTATE PLANNING

Regardless of your age, stage in life, or amount of assets, you need to plan your estate. You might be wealthy or not, single or married, working or retired. In every case, proper estate planning is a must if you want to maintain control over your personal matters and assets during your lifetime and after you pass away. Without proper planning, you not only forfeit control over important decisions, but the administration of your estate can become complicated and expensive.

While you're still alive, your estate plan should document your intentions and transfer assets to people or trusts that you choose. The plan should—in the event that you become incapacitated—appoint a guardian to care for your children, a person to make medical decisions for you, and an individual to make financial decisions on your behalf.

Your plan also should provide directives to be followed after your death—such as distributing your assets when, how, and to whom you choose; providing charitable gifts to organizations; transferring your business interests according to a succession plan; and appointing a guardian to care for your children. The plan can further help your loved ones by minimizing potential expenses and taxes, avoiding legal and financial complications and delays, and preventing family disputes.

Even if you have created an estate plan, constant changes in tax law might prompt you to re-evaluate and update your plan in light of those changes.

Where's the money?

Proper estate planning must address the issue of liquidity to pay expenses. You may not leave behind enough cash to pay federal and state estate taxes, which will be due within nine months of your death; and probate and funeral expenses can be significant. As a result, your beneficiaries may need to sell assets below fair market value to generate cash quickly, leading to family disputes over assets that have shared ownership. If your beneficiaries borrow the needed money, they will have to pay interest in addition to principal, using after-tax dollars.

Planning for incapacity

In many cases, if you become unable to make decisions for yourself and have not prepared the documents listed below, decisions will be made for you by law, or a person will be appointed by the court to make decisions for you. After creating the following documents, you should discuss these decisions with your family and other named persons; and provide medically-related documents to your primary care physician.

Durable power of attorney—A *durable power of attorney* is a legal document in which you (the *principal*) are appointing the person or persons (*attorney-in-fact*) that you want to make financial decisions for you. In this document, you must specify the powers being granted and when the document becomes effective. This document should be created by an attorney and customized to meet your needs.

Health care proxy—Also referred to as an *advance health care directive* or *medical power of attorney*, this document appoints a person (*health care agent*) to make health care decisions for you if you are unable to do so. This document also serves as a directive for the appointed person, or to limit your health care agent's power.

Living will—A living will specifically documents your wishes about being kept alive in case of a terminal illness or persistent unconsciousness.

Income taxes

If your estate plan does not minimize the taxes that must be paid upon your death, your spouse's standard of living may sink like a stone, and your heirs may be forced to borrow money or sell assets to pay estate taxes—which would be due within 9 months of your death.

But that's not all. Following your death, income taxes would be due on any income you earned during the year of your death, income earned by your estate after your death but before all your assets are distributed, and *income in respect of a decedent*—which would include pre-tax contributions or tax-deferred earnings from accounts such as IRAs, retirement plans, or tax-deferred annuities.

Capital gains taxes

An *appreciated asset* is one that has a higher market value than its book value or taxable value and which, upon its sale, will generate a capital gain. When transferring appreciated assets, capital gains taxes differ depending upon whether you gift them during your lifetime or leave them in your will. When appreciated assets are gifted prior to death, the person receiving the gift and then selling it will owe capital gains on the entire increase in value between what was originally paid and the sale price. But when appreciated assets are inherited, their basis may be stepped up—which means that your beneficiaries may owe capital gains only on any increase in the asset value from the time of inheritance until the time when the asset is sold.

Transfer taxes

Transfer taxes are taxes on the passing of title to property from one person or entity to another. They are essentially transaction fees imposed on the transfer of title to property. There are four basic kinds:

Gift tax—The *gift tax* is a federal tax that may be owed, when you die, if you give money or assets without receiving fair compensation. Gift taxes are owed only on gifts that exceed both an annual limit per recipient and a lifetime gift tax exemption that changes each year. In addition, only gifts that exceed the annual limit reduce the lifetime limit! Gifts given to a charity or spouse are generally exempt from this tax. If someone gives $100,000 to any one person, it only reduces their lifetime gift amount by that amount, minus the "free amount". As an example let's assume your lifetime exemption is $5,200,000, and the most you can give in one year, without reducing your lifetime amount, is $14,000 and you give away $114,000. The first $14,000 is free, the next $100,000 goes against the $5,200,000; so now you only have $5,100,000 left to give – so what? Most people get too worked up about the annual limits and don't focus on the lifetime limits.

Federal estate tax—The *federal estate tax* may be placed upon your estate at the time of death based on the value of your taxable estate. Assets left to a charity or spouse are exempt from this tax.

Generation-skipping transfer tax—The *generation-skipping transfer tax* can be imposed on a gift or inheritance to persons at least two generations younger than the person making the transfer. This tax has an exemption, which under current law is equal to the estate tax *applicable exclusion amount,* which is the value of the taxable estate that can pass free of transfer taxes. The applicable exclusion amount changes annually.

State inheritance or estate taxes—Several states have *inheritance or estate taxes* that are owed in addition to the federal tax. State rules and rates vary greatly and may not mimic the federal program. You should consult with an estate planning attorney to determine if you may be subject to these taxes.

Portability

Portability is an estate planning concept that was first introduced in a 2010 federal law and extended indefinitely in 2012. Portability allows a surviving spouse to take advantage of the unused portion of the estate tax applicable exclusion amount of his or her predeceased spouse. This would provide the surviving spouse with a larger exclusion amount.

Portability will reduce the estate tax for many people but it also has several limitations. Before planning to use portability provisions, you should consult with an estate planning attorney.

How to calculate your taxable estate

Your *taxable estate* will determine how much you may owe in federal and state estate taxes. To calculate your taxable estate, you must first add your estate's assets—using their fair market value—to determine your *gross estate*. Estate assets include not only assets owned solely by you, but half of the assets you own jointly with your spouse, your percentage of assets owned jointly with anyone else, and your percentage of any business or partnership you partially own. Assets might also include such things as survivor income benefits; debts owed to you; annuity and life insurance death benefits, and retirement plan benefits.

Next, you need to add your estate's *liabilities and expenses* to determine your *allowable deductions*. Liabilities and expense include things like taxes you owe, estate settlement costs, outstanding debts, funeral expenses, and assets you leave to your spouse.

Finally, subtract your allowable deductions from your gross estate to determine the value of your taxable estate.

Your will

A will is an important legal document because it outlines how your estate will be distributed when you die, and appoints a person or entity—called an *executor* or *personal representative*—to administer your estate. But it's important to remember that you might wish to change your will at some point in the future due to such things as marriage, divorce, the death of your beneficiary or executor, the birth of a child, one of your children reaching age 18, a change in your wealth, a move to a different state, new legislation, or a change of mind about your executor or beneficiary. Even if you don't experience any of these major life changes, it's a good idea to review your will every few years to make sure it accurately reflects your wishes and if you want to protect the heirs of your heirs (like your grandchildren), insist the language "per issue" or "per stirpes" be put into your Will; so if one of your beneficiaries dies before you do, their share will go to their "next of kin".

Dying without a will

If you die without a will, referred to as *dying intestate*, some of your assets will be transferred directly, but a probate judge will distribute your remaining assets according to the intestate succession laws in your state of residence. Each state has laws that direct what happens to property when you die without a valid will. Generally, only spouses, blood relatives and in some states registered domestic partners can inherit assets under intestate succession laws; while unmarried partners, friends, and charities get nothing. If the deceased person was married, the surviving spouse usually gets the largest share.

Needless to say, when you die without a will you lose control over your personal decisions—such as how, when and to whom your assets will be distributed. Here are some of the specific problems that can occur if you die intestate:

- A person or entity will be appointed to administer your estate.

- A guardian will be appointed for your minor children.
- All your children will be treated equally, regardless of their needs or your wishes.
- If your children inherit some of your assets, the court will appoint a conservator to manage those assets until the children receive them at age 18.
- Distant relatives may receive assets that you intended to leave to your friends or favorite charities.
- Depending on the law in your state, all your assets may go to your spouse and none to your children from a previous marriage.
- Depending upon state law, no assets may go to your unmarried partner.
- Your estate may incur taxes and expenses that could have been avoided.
- Your estate may experience delays and a shortage of liquid assets to pay the estate taxes that will be due within 9 months of your death.

Is a will all you need?

Having a will allows you to select the person or entity you want to carry out the terms of your will, the persons or organizations (*beneficiaries*) you want to receive your assets, and a guardian for your minor children. A will also enables you to specify any limitations pertaining to when and how your assets will be distributed and any assets you want to be transferred into trusts upon your death; and it guarantees the administration of your estate will be supervised by the probate court.

But there are some distinct disadvantages to a "will-only" estate plan. To determine if your will is valid, it will be subjected to probate, and that can be costly. Your will can be challenged, your creditors can make claims on your estate, and your assets will not be available to your heirs until your estate is approved by probate court—a process that usually takes 6 months to more than 2 years. What's more, all information about your assets will become available to the public.

Probate

Probate is a legal process that identifies the value of what you own and distributes your assets after your death. Some say it's an announcement to the World, "if I die, does anyone have a claim against my stuff"? If you don't have a will, all your assets subject to probate will be distributed according to state law. If you do have a will, probate will supervise the execution of your will's instructions.

The good thing about probate is that it provides a consistent legal process for handling your estate following your death. It determines the validity of your will and interprets its intent, provides court supervision to ensure your executor is acting according to your will, and generally limits the time in which the will can be challenged and creditors can make claims on the estate. It pays any of your debts and taxes, settles disputes, and transfers legal title—and doesn't influence any assets transferred by other methods.

But probate has some major drawbacks. Probate-related fees and expenses usually average between 3 and 8 percent of the value of the probated estate, and—as we stated earlier—your assets subject to probate may not be available to your beneficiaries or heirs during the probate period, and all the information about your assets will become available to the public.

How to avoid probate

Due to the time, expense and publicity associated with probate, many people take advantage of strategies that can be used to transfer many of their assets outside of probate by giving them to family members or even friends. This allows you to witness a loved-one enjoying your gift while you're still alive, and reduces the size of your estate and estate taxes. You'll owe gift taxes only on gifts that exceed both the annual limit and the lifetime gift tax exclusion.

The downside to making gifts during your lifetime is that it forces you to forfeit any income from the gifted asset; any potential price appreciation of the asset; and control of how or when the asset will be used.

There is another way to avoid probate, and that is through *joint tenancy with rights of survivorship,* a type of ownership in which two or more people hold ownership of property as joint tenants. The property will avoid probate until the death of the final survivor.

But there are some distinct disadvantages to this type of joint ownership. For one thing, the deceased person's ownership interest in the property is automatically inherited by the other owner or owners, regardless of instructions in the deceased person's will or living trust. Other drawbacks are that you can't place restrictions on the survivors, you might unintentionally disinherit your heirs, and you have no protection from potential estate taxes. And before your death, other owners will have access to the jointly-owned asset, the property may be subject to the claims of other owners' creditors, and you may face potential gift tax liability.

Joint ownership

In addition to *joint tenancy with rights of survivorship*, there are three other types of joint ownership, none of which will allow the owners to avoid probate. The property being held by two or more people could be things like real estate, a business, bank accounts, or stock. Here are the three types:

Tenancy by the entirety—This is a somewhat outdated type of joint ownership, but it's still allowed in many states. It provides right of survivorship, and is available only to a husband and his wife. One advantage is that the residence is protected from the claims of either the husband's or wife's creditors, but it's not protected from joint creditors.

Tenants in common—When two or more people own property as *tenants in common*—meaning two or more people possess the property simultaneously—the deceased's ownership is not automatically inherited by the other owners. Rather, it is included in the deceased's estate and distributed accordingly.

Community property—If you live in 1 of 9 *community property* states—In which the surviving spouse has rights to the deceased spouse's 401(k) assets regardless of the named beneficiary unless the spouse has waived all rights to the account in writing—the property acquired by either spouse or both spouses during the marriage is presumed to be community property unless it was acquired as separate property by gift or inheritance. The deceased spouse's 50 percent interest in the community property is included in his or her estate and distributed accordingly. If it's held as community property, the deceased spouse's community property interest gets a *step-up* in basis to the date-of-death value, and the surviving spouse's community interest also gets an equal step-up.

Direct transfer assets

Direct transfer assets are assets that can be automatically transferred to your loved ones without having them go through probate and its associated expenses. But it's important to be aware that direct transfer assets are not available for all types of assets, and can create problems if you name minors or people who are incapacitated to receive the assets. Assets can be directly transferred through *beneficiary designations* or *payable on death accounts*:

Beneficiary designations—Certain types of assets—such as insurance policies, annuities, IRA and Roth IRA accounts and 401(k) accounts—allow you to name a beneficiary. Since the beneficiary will automatically receive the asset upon your death, the asset will avoid probate. It is important to periodically review any beneficiary designations to make sure they accurately reflect your wishes.

Payable on death accounts—A *payable on death registration* allows the ownership of certain assets to pass automatically to the person you name without the risks associated with joint ownership. The transfer of these assets—things like bank accounts, certificates of deposit, mutual fund accounts, and brokerage accounts—avoids probate.

Trusts

A trust is a legal entity that can be created to hold title to assets, as well as manage and distribute them, according to specific terms and conditions. Depending on what type of trust you establish, it can:

- Avoid probate and publicity.
- Isolate and transfer assets even if your will is contested.
- Equalize inheritances.
- Distribute indivisible property among beneficiaries.
- Simplify the distribution of certain assets, such as property you own in a different state.
- Protect assets from creditors' claims or lawsuits.
- Manage assets for a beneficiary who can't handle financial responsibility.
- Delay the transfer of ownership or possession of assets until a certain time or event.
- Transfer the responsibility of managing assets.
- Plan for the possibility of incapacity.
- Minimize or avoid income, gift, and potential estate taxes.

There are five basic types of trusts:

TESTAMENTARY TRUSTS

Testamentary trusts are created by your will and are funded by your estate. These trusts are administered by the *trustee* or *trustees*—one or more parties who hold title to the trust's assets and administer the trust according to specified terms and conditions—that you name in your will. Since the trusts don't go into effect until after you pass away, they enable you to own and manage your assets during your lifetime.

REVOCABLE LIVING TRUSTS

Grantors often use revocable living trusts not only to avoid probate, but to maintain flexibility and control over their assets during their lifetime. All assets should be transferred and owned in the name of the trust, and a *pour over will* can be used to transfer any assets outside your trust into your trust upon your death.

These trusts enable you to hold assets in multiple states and avoid multiple probates; reduce the risk of your will being contested; and make changes to the terms, trustees, or beneficiaries in case you change your mind or want to adjust to legislative changes. They also might contain provisions designed to save married couples from paying potential estate taxes.

When you die the trust's assets can be distributed to the beneficiaries designated in your trust according to the specified time frame, or they may be held in further trust for their benefit. But revocable living trusts do not save income taxes, and are not protected from your creditors.

IRREVOCABLE TRUSTS

As its name implies, once an *irrevocable trust* is created, it can't be revoked or modified by the grantor. Though irrevocable trusts force the grantor to surrender control of the trust and its assets, they are often used to minimize or avoid income taxes and potential estate taxes. Common types of irrevocable trusts are *irrevocable life insurance trusts* and *charitable remainder trusts*.

IRREVOCABLE LIFE INSURANCE TRUSTS

You can set up an *irrevocable life insurance trust* during your lifetime to avoid probate and shelter life insurance benefits from potential estate taxes. Since the trust owns the insurance policy and death benefits are paid to the trust, these assets will avoid probate and the claims of creditors. But since this trust is irrevocable, the grantor must give up rights to the trust's assets; and cannot revoke or change the terms of the trust or change the beneficiaries. Any assets or insurance policies transferred to the trust may be subject to a gift tax.

If the trust purchases the life insurance policy, there may be immediate protection from potential estate taxes. The death benefit can be excluded from your estate, meaning no taxes will be owed, and money will be available to pay for your estate expenses. But if you transfer an existing policy into the trust, the insurance proceeds may be subject to estate taxes if you die within three years of the transfer.

CHARITABLE REMAINER TRUSTS

A *charitable remainder trust* can serve the dual purpose of providing a gift to a qualifying charity of your choice and generating a source of income for you. The income stream will be paid at least annually for your lifetime, you and your spouse's joint lifetime, or your chosen beneficiary's lifetime. They can also help you avoid potential estate taxes, gift taxes, and probate.

A charitable income tax deduction, based on the estimated value of assets expected to pass to the charity at your death, is available for the year in which you set up the trust and contribute assets to it. Upon your death or your beneficiary's death, all the trust's assets will be transferred to the charity you've selected. If assets held in trust are sold, no capital gains are due upon the sale since the trust is tax exempt. Capital gains will be taxable to a non-charitable beneficiary if the assets are distributed later.

David Hays   Doug Hughes

ABOUT THE AUTHORS

David Hays is the founder, president and senior consultant of Comprehensive Financial Consultants, Inc. (CFC). His firm was chartered to deliver financial planning and investment advice to individuals, businesses, retirement plans and not-for-profit organizations in 1994.

In 2003, Comprehensive Financial Consultants Institutional (CFCI) was formed. CFCI is an SEC Registered Investment Advisor.

The staff of CFC and CFCI includes five financial consultants, a fixed-income portfolio manager, an equity portfolio manager, an insurance consultant, an operations manager, a marketing assistant, and four administrative assistants.

David is co-author of "Today's Guide to Retirement Planning." He hosts the weekly radio show "Your Money with David Hays" on AM1370, FM98.7 out of Bloomington, Indiana. He has taught retirement planning courses through Indiana University School of Continuing Studies and Ivy Tech Community College. David serves as a U.S. Congressional Advisor on the topics of Medicare, taxes, and retirement planning issues. He has been a guest speaker for a variety of local and national organizations, discussing economic and investment trends. David has assisted with and been quoted in several newspapers and magazines, including The *Wall Street Journal* and *Kiplinger's Personal Finance* magazine. He also spoke at the Harvard Faculty Club in 2016 on getting America retirement ready.

David attended Greenville College in 1988, where he played football. He then transferred to Indiana University in 1989 and finished his education at The Indiana University School of Business in December of 1993, with a concentration in accounting. He continues being educated in the area of tax and retirement planning, by being a member of the Ed Slott Elite IRA Advisor Group. David was given the 2018 Miracle Maker Award from the Children's Organ Transplant Association (COTA), he's a proud board member of both the Boys & Girls Club of Bloomington as well as Monroe County CASA (Court Appointed Special Advocates).

David and his wife, Misti, have been married since 1993 and have one son, William.

Doug Hughes joined the Comprehensive Financial Consultants Team in July 2003 and is the Vice President of Comprehensive Financial Consultants and an investment consultant. Doug's primary responsibility is overseeing client accounts and helping to shape their savings for the future.

A big believer in creating financial freedom for oneself, he concentrates on creating this for his clients so they can feel confident in their financial situation. Doug prides himself on being available to his clients and aims to provide premier service regardless of their wealth. To that end, he will make sure he is informed about a client's investments and will often take part in several continuing education courses offered throughout the year to stay up-to-date on industry trends.

A strong believer in the power of education, Hughes co-hosts classes at Ivy Tech Community that are geared towards financial readiness for retirement. These classes simplify complex concepts so that the average person preparing to retire can fully understand their options. He was also a visiting lecturer at Indiana University's School of Public and Environmental Affairs, teaching courses on personal finances.

A native of Bloomington, Indiana, Doug Hughes received his Bachelor's degree in Theology from Indiana Bible College. After graduation, Doug began working in the financial services industry. His first two years were served as an office administrator, and then he began working as an investment broker.

Doug continues educating team members at several local organizations, businesses and non-profit groups, including Baxter Pharmaceuticals, Duke Energy, IU Continuing Studies and the Girl Scouts of America. Doug has been, and continues to be, heavily involved with a local affiliate of Business Network International, since joining in 2001.

Hughes is married to his wife Terri, with whom he shares one child, Daniel, born in 2004. Together they are members of the Family Life Worship Center where Doug also volunteers by providing financial education seminars to the congregation. In his free time, Doug is an avid fisherman and reader, enjoys traveling on cruises with his wife Terri, and frequents art galleries and museums both locally and during his travels.

www.ingramcontent.com/pod-product-compliance
Lightning Source LLC
Chambersburg PA
CBHW020657220526
45464CB00001B/478